entrepreneur
PRIME

entrepreneurprime.co.uk
Issue 4 II 2024
GLOBAL EDITION

£24.90 II $29.90 II €27.90

INTERV...
GO...
Azure...
SUS...
Aut...
of...

Exclusive Insights
Talks with Visionary Entrepreneurs!

DR. DERRY McIVOR
Navigates the Future

OLYMPIA THEOFANOPOULO...
Promotes Greek Magic Worldwide

CHRIS MASLI...
Empowering business transitions

HEIDI ELLERT-McDERMOTT
Transforms Speechwriting

An interview with
DR. HUGO DE LA PEÑA
Conquering Cancer?
Story of Hope, Resilience and Triumph

available at

Dive
Into a Great Journey

Ready to
share
your
story?

Reader's House
London's Literary Gateway

readershouse.co.uk

What Exceptional Leadership Looks Like
Top Motivational Speaker
Rocky Romanella
Discusses Leadership Expectations, Values And Character

Renowned as a keynote speaker, trainer, and Forbes Contributor, Romanella founded 3SIXTY Management Services, LLC. With 40+ years in leadership, he served as CEO and Director at UniTek Global Services after a 36-year UPS career.

WILMINGTON, NC /24-7PressRelease

In today's rapidly evolving landscape, the essence of leadership extends far beyond boardrooms and political arenas. Every facet of society, from parents to educators, holds a leadership role, shaping the fabric of our communities. Understanding the essence of exceptional leadership is paramount, and renowned motivational speaker Rocky Romanella sheds light on this critical aspect.

Romanella, a distinguished keynote speaker, trainer, and Forbes Contributor, brings over 40 years of leadership experience to the forefront. As the founder of 3SIXTY Management Services, LLC, and having served as CEO and Director at UniTek Global Services, his insights resonate deeply in various spheres.

In a recent article featured on his website, Romanella delves into the fundamental principles of exceptional leadership. He emphasizes the importance of setting clear expectations for leaders within organizations. These expectations, intertwined with values and workplace policies, serve as guiding beacons, illuminating the path toward exemplary leadership.

Romanella advocates for a proactive approach wherein leaders not only embody these expectations but also encourage their teams to internalize and uphold them. By fostering alignment and commitment, leaders can cultivate a culture of excellence and integrity within their organizations.

Central to Romanella's philosophy are the core values that underpin every successful enterprise. Integrity, excellence, and a commitment to fostering a conducive work environment form the bedrock upon which thriving organizations are built. Through balanced leadership and unwavering adherence to these values, companies can transcend challenges and achieve sustained success.

Romanella's article elucidates a comprehensive framework for aspiring leaders, offering actionable insights and strategies to navigate the complexities of leadership effectively. By embracing change, fostering collaboration, and celebrating success, individuals can elevate their leadership prowess and make a lasting impact in their respective domains.

For the full article and a myriad of resources tailored for leaders across industries, visit the 3Sixty Management Services website at https://3sixtymanagementservices.com. Discover the transformative power of exceptional leadership and embark on a journey towards personal and professional growth under the guidance of Rocky Romanella.

PHOTO: *Renowned motivational speaker and leadership expert, Rocky Romanella, shares insights into the essence of exceptional leadership, guiding individuals towards personal and professional growth.*

IN THIS ISSUE

8

ON THE COVER

Conquering Cancer?
Collaborations and Initiatives for Global Impact

An Interview with
DR. HUGODELAPEÑA

"Dr. Hugo De La Peña, an eminent oncologist and innovator, shares insights on revolutionizing cancer care through pioneering research, compassionate patient support, and relentless dedication to curing cancer."

"Dr. Terry Mcivor, founder of IGH3P®, pioneers PNLPsy™, integrating NLP, psychology, and neuroscience. Empirical validation and ethical integrity define his approach, shaping the future of coaching and mental health support globally."

EDITOR'S LETTER

In this fourth issue of Entrepreneur Prime magazine, we celebrate the audacity of visionaries who are not just navigating uncharted territories but are also redrawing the maps of their respective fields. Their stories are more than narratives of personal triumph; they represent a beacon for aspiring entrepreneurs and innovators worldwide.

Our cover features Dr. Hugo De La Peña, a name that has become synonymous with ground-breaking advancements in cancer care. Dr. De La Peña's pioneering work in oncology is not just a testament to his exceptional skill and intellect but also to his profound compassion for those he serves. His innovative approaches to treatment and his advocacy for cancer research funding are reshaping the landscape of healthcare, offering new hope where once there was little. His presence on our cover reflects the ethos of Entrepreneur Prime: to spotlight leaders who are making a tangible, positive impact on the world.

In keeping with our tradition of featuring game-changers, we also had the honour of interviewing Dr. Terry McIvor, President and Founder of the International Guild of Hypnotherapy, NLP, and 3 Principles Practitioners and Trainers (IGH3P). Dr. McIvor's ground-breaking work in Patho-physiological Neuro-Linguistic Psychology (PNLPsy™) is pioneering a new era in psychological sciences. His approach integrates neuro-linguistic programming, empirical psychology, and neuroscience to forge PNLPsy™, an innovative framework that holds the potential to revolutionise coaching, mentoring, and therapeutic practices.

Ramon Gras Alomà, a pioneering City Science researcher and co-founder at Aretian Urban Analytics and Design, applies cutting-edge methodologies and academic rigor to revolutionise urban design. His work offers transformative insights for sustainable development in the face of technological evolution.

But our exploration of visionary entrepreneurship does not end here. We have also conducted interviews with other remarkable entrepreneurs whose diverse ventures are united by a common thread: the drive to initiate change.

Olympia Theofanopoulou, through her brand OLIA Scarves, weaves the rich tapestry of Greek culture into every silk thread, marrying tradition with contemporary aesthetics. Her dedication to quality and cultural expression exemplifies how entrepreneurship can serve as a bridge between history and modernity, local craftsmanship and global markets.

Chris Maslin's GoEO represents another facet of entrepreneurship's vast landscape. With a focus on eco-friendly travel experiences, Maslin's venture is a testament to the growing importance of sustainability in business models. His work serves as a reminder that profitability and environmental stewardship can go hand-in-hand.

Heidi Ellert-McDermott's story, while distinct, is equally inspiring. Her journey underscores the power of creativity and the importance of adapting to market needs, proving that entrepreneurial success often requires a willingness to pivot and persist through adversity.

Each entrepreneur we've interviewed brings a unique perspective on what it means to innovate and lead in today's rapidly evolving business world. Their stories are not just narratives of success; they are blueprints for impact, imbued with lessons for all who aspire to make their mark.

As you turn the pages of this issue, we invite you to draw inspiration from these pioneers. Let their journeys enlighten your path, their challenges fortify your resolve, and their successes broaden your vision of what is possible.

At Entrepreneur Prime, we believe that entrepreneurship is about more than starting businesses; it's about starting movements.

Enjoy reading

Acacia Baldie

PUBLISHER
Entrepreneur Pirme
A Subsidiary of
Newyox.Media

200 Suite
134-146 Curtain Road
EC2A 3AR London
t: +44 79 3847 8420

editor@entrepreneurprime.co.uk
https://entrepreneurprime.co.uk

EDITORIAL
Acacia Baldie
editor@entrepreneurprime.co.uk
AJ. Somer
interview@entrepreneurprime.co.uk
Ben Alan
ben.alan@entrepreneurprime.co.uk

entrepreneur prime

Empowers Globally

newyox.media

Conquering Cancer?
Collaborations and Initiatives for Global Impact

An Interview with
DR. HUGO DE LA PEÑA

"Dr. Hugo De La Peña, an eminent oncologist and innovator, shares insights on revolutionizing cancer care through pioneering research, compassionate patient support, and relentless dedication to curing cancer."

BY ACACIA BALDIE | LONDON

Dr. Hugo De La Peña stands as a beacon of innovation and dedication in the realm of cancer care. An esteemed Medical Oncology Consultant within the NHS, Dr. De La Peña's journey is not merely a career but a lifelong commitment to combating one of humanity's most formidable adversaries: cancer.

Dr. Hugo De La Peña: A Trailblazer in Cancer Care

Explore the journey of Dr. Hugo De La Peña, a visionary oncologist dedicated to redefining the battle against cancer. From pioneering immunotherapy to advocating for patient support, his story inspires hope.

Born with an insatiable drive for discovery, Dr. De La Peña's academic journey began with distinction, graduating at the apex of his class from Medical School with unparalleled academic honours. His thirst for knowledge propelled him across continents, culminating in a PhD in Cancer Genetics and Tumour Immunology from University College London, where his ground-breaking research in cancer vaccines garnered international acclaim, earning him the coveted Young Scientist Award.

Throughout his illustrious career, Dr. De La Peña has been a trailblazer, challenging conventional wisdom and pioneering novel approaches to cancer treatment. His relentless pursuit of understanding the intricate dynamics between the immune system and cancer has led to paradigm shifts in oncological therapeutics. Through a fusion of rigorous research and compassionate patient care, Dr. De La Peña has elevated the standard of cancer treatment, earning him recognition as a Fellow of the Royal College of Physicians.

In our exclusive interview with Entrepreneur Prime magazine, Dr. De La Peña unveils the insights and inspirations that have shaped his remarkable journey. From the challenges of navigating the arduous path to consultancy to the transformative power of immunotherapy, Dr. De La Peña offers invaluable wisdom for aspiring entrepreneurs and healthcare pioneers alike.

Beyond his clinical endeavours, Dr. Peña's impact reverberates across diverse spheres, from his role as a Cancer Research UK Ambassador to his commitment as a Maggie's Clinical Lead, ensuring holistic support for cancer patients and their families.

As we delve into Dr. De La Peña's narrative, we glimpse the essence of his mission: to redefine the narrative of cancer from one of despair to one of hope, resilience, and relentless pursuit of a cure.

Join us as we embark on a journey through the mind and heart of Dr. Hugo De La Peña, a visionary entrepreneur whose unwavering resolve is reshaping the landscape of cancer care.

What inspired you to start your business career?

For me curing cancer is not a business, is my life's commitment. Killing cancer for a living gives me immeasurable satisfaction and it is the best thing I could ever have dreamed of doing. Cancer will affect 1 in 2 of us in our lifetime, so very early on in life, I decided I had one of two choices: either bury my head in the sand and hope it will never happen to me or tackle it, prevent it from happening if I can or prepare to beat it when my turn comes. Cancer is a brutal disease, make no mistake, and the devastation it causes is physical, mental and economical at a monumental level. I learnt that as a teenager and it was the brutality I witnessed what made me study medicine as the path to become a cancer killing specialist.

What challenges did you find at the beginning of your journey and how did you overcome them?

The main challenge was the time it takes to reach consultancy, that is when you can finally plan and directly drive clinical trials and make treatment decisions. It took 7 years of medical school, 10 years of research and 4 years of specialty. Most friends my age were making serious money when I was on call at weekends or nights studying for exit exams. So patience really is a virtue and envy of what others are already doing has no

Continued *on page 10*

"**Dr. Hugo De La Peña: Dr. Hugo De La Peña, MD, PHD, FRCP, a pioneer in cancer care, brings innovation and compassion to the forefront of oncological**

Dr. Hugo De La Peña: Innovator in oncology, revolutionizing cancer care with pioneering immunotherapy, holistic patient support, and relentless scientific pursuit.

place. To overcome challenges, you just have to keep working hard because you know payback will come once you are out of the tunnel, as long as you know exactly how long the tunnel is. Do please surround yourself of people that are either cleverer than you or experts in other areas, some of them (not all) will help you later on. Be nice to people, you have no idea how many doors that will open to you when you least expect it. Envy from others is inevitable, but pay no attention, easier said than done, but if you are doing what you are doing with hard work, integrity and makes you happy, you have already won.

How did you get the idea for your business research and why did you think it would work?

Cancer cure rates were 25% when I was born (in the 70s), they are 50% now (2020s) and in the next 10 years they will be 75%. So I knew early on increasing cancer cure rates was truly a priority and unmet need for mankind. Companies and scientist to an extent, put most of their money in gene therapy projects, which many thought would be the magic bullet for most diseases including cancer. Genetic engineering has become a wonderful tool, but gene therapy hasn't been the golden bullet people thought it would be. I bet instead in using the immune system to kill cancers and I concentrated in immunotherapy before it became the (good) monster it is now and before it was given the Nobel prize in 2018. We were taught at medical school that cancers were invisible to the immune system because cancers come from self and our immune systems are trained not to recognise us as foreign. That is something I never believed. I always challenged that idea as I already knew some leukaemias could be cured using the immune system. Going against the "status quo" is always hard, especially as a student because no one will take you seriously; challenging what "we know for a fact" is never popular. I also knew malignant transformation is a common occurrence in all of us, it happens almost daily and our immune systems deal with that. I just needed to prove it. It is clear now and widely accepted that the immune system is the most powerful cancer killing machinery

known to man and all the sceptics have now jumped into the bang wagon. The fact we cure more cancers now and we have started to cure the (previously) incurable cancers has made immunotherapy the first line treatment for most cancers. I therefore say immunotherapy is simply better than sliced bread.

What kind of research did you do before you started?

I have been doing research literally all my life, from thinking and overthinking why cancers are on the rise, to having spent over 10 years (PH and Postdocs) doing translational research directly analysing human behaviour and creating scientific platforms to kill cancers using the immune system. I am still not done and keep focused in understanding how the immune system kills cancer and how we can still tune immunotherapy strategies to kill cancers without toxicity. I am still doing research by collaborating with universities providing vital real cancer samples so that we can understand cancer biology better.

How did you raise the money to start your business?

Knowledge is money, after finishing medical school, I had to convince the Mexican Government to pay for my PHD in London and they funded my PHD fully, knowledge again (put on paper) won me hundreds of thousands of pounds from Cancer Charities to fund my postdoctoral research projects. That is incredibly stressful, but is how scientists generate, earn and make money to keep going. You don't do this single handed, that is why it is so important to surround yourself of mentors and a good team(s) where organic collaborations become formal and everyone wins.

What makes your business unique?

The relentless hunger to cure people. I can make people happy by giving them their life back. Many cancers happen for no reason at all, no one is at fault, most of my patients don't smoke, don't drink, are not overweight and have a healthy lifestyle and yet cancer "just happens". So when we cure those cancers, we give life back. Some other cancers are preventable when they are caused by smoking, excessive alcohol drinking and irresponsible sun exposure for example, so when we cure those cancers, we give people a 2nd chance at

"If you work hard and you are honest, you will ALWAYS do well."

living and again, if I have to accept that a cancer cannot be cured, then we aim to buy precious time for those patients.

What advice would you give to someone who is trying to become an entrepreneur?

Do your homework, if your idea is sound, stick to your guns and go for it. If you work hard and you are honest, you will ALWAYS do well. Be nice to people, you will be surprised how many doors that simple gesture will open for you. Don't quit if you fail, failure is part of success and try hard to ignore envy, that you will face for sure.

How did you market your business?

I let International Clinical Trials "market" my practice. Private medicine is full of charlatans and the word Cancer brings panic and desperation to patients and relatives. Some people take advantage of that fear and make a killing with shameful, unethical promises and unproven treatments, so I am always very careful not to give false hope, but equally, don't take it away either. Every treatment decision I make is based on evidence to back me up and protect myself as well. It's about being honest and making sure you go to bed with a clean conscience, but I don't hide facts from patients, if its good news I tell them, but if it's bad news, I also tell them straight.

What daily habits do you use to help you succeed?

30 protected minutes every day to release stress, chronic stress is the source of all evil, chronic stress dampens your immune system and that increase your chances of having/de-

DR. HUGO DE LA PEÑA

Dr. Hugo De La Peña's tireless dedication to cancer care embodies the epitome of excellence and compassion. As a pioneering force in oncology, his groundbreaking research in immunotherapy has revolutionized treatment paradigms, offering new hope to patients worldwide. His commitment to holistic patient support and relentless pursuit of scientific advancement herald a new era in the fight against cancer, earning him admiration and gratitude on a global scale.

veloping cancer, chronic stress will also affect your personal and work relationships alongside your mental health. Have some protected "me time" daily, very difficult I know, but the best ideas I have ever had happen when I am walking or running on my own.

What do you most enjoy about working for yourself?

Seeing cancers melt away because of my treatment plans is the most enjoyable and gratifying part of my job, giving patients their life back is a pretty amazing thing to do and gives me work purpose. I teach and teach every time I can, I teach secondary school children and the general public about cancer prevention (40% of cancers are preventable) and the risks around smoking, vaping, excessive alcohol drinking, irresponsible sun exposure and being overweight. I teach how to kill and prevent cancer to medical students, doctors, registrars and consultants because the more of us we are out there, the worse it gets for cancer.

What plans do you have for the future?

As NHS Cancer Consultant my ongoing and future job is to treat as many cancer patients as possible making sure we have access to clinical trials so that we can keep increasing our cure and survival rates.

As a CRUK Ambassador my ongoing and future job is to create awareness about the preventable causes of cancer at local and national level by talking to as many kids, adults and ministers as possible at organised events. I also raised funds relentlessly to support cancer research projects, because the more research there is, the less cancer there is as well.

As a Royal College of Physicians Chief SPR Mentor, my ongoing and future job is to inspire and advice junior doctors to get involved in top level management projects to change and improve our NHS management and service delivery strategies.

As Maggie's Clinical Lead, my ongoing and future job is to make sure we offer medically sound and evidence-based support to cancer patients as soon as the diagnosis of cancer is being given, but the support is also for the relatives who find navigating the diagnosis of cancer in a loved one just as hard.

EXITS: Embracing Life's Transience Through Poetry's Eloquent Tapestry

Stephen C. Pollock's Masterpiece Explores Mortality, Renewal, and the Beauty of Human Experience

"Exits, a masterful fusion of poetic brilliance and profound introspection, captures life's essence with evocative verses and captivating imagery."

Exits," penned by Stephen C. Pollock, is a poignant exploration of life's ephemerality, resonating with the essence of mortality and the potential for renewal. Drawing upon nature's imagery and metaphors, Pollock weaves a tapestry of verses that delve deep into the human experience.

This collection is a testament to Pollock's mastery, showcasing a diverse array of poetic styles, ranging from traditional forms to the expressive freedom of free verse, even extending to hybrid creations. The inclusion of accompanying artwork enriches the reader's journey and harmonizes with the written word to amplify its impact.

> *"Pollock's poetry is brilliant. The exploration of form is thoroughly enjoyable and inspiring. Many of Pollock's pieces are reminiscent of Irish poets like Eavan Boland and Seamus Heaney."*
>
> **— Kristiana Reed,**
> Editor-in-Chief, Free Verse Revolution

The accolades and awards that adorn "Exits" are a testament to its brilliance. Garnering the Gold Medal for poetry in the Readers' Favorite 2023 International Book Awards and receiving recognition in literary journals and competitions, this collection stands tall among contemporary works. Its impact reverberates within the literary realm, earning acclaim and admiration from critics and fellow poets alike.

Reviewers have lauded Pollock's craftsmanship, drawing parallels to revered poets like Seamus Heaney and likening the artistry of some pieces to Shakespearean sonnets. Kristiana Reed,

EXITS

Stephen C. Pollock

Selected Poems

Editor-in-Chief of Free Verse Revolution, finds Pollock's work reminiscent of the great Irish poets, while IndieReader praises the formal poems as artful and masterful, comparable to the works of renowned literary figures.

The collection's embrace of life's beauty and fragility echoes throughout the verses, showcasing a musicality of language that captivates and moves its readers. Pollock's poems exude intelligence and poignancy, leaving an indelible mark on anyone who delves into this exquisite volume.

"Exits" is not merely a book of poetry; it's a profound reflection on existence, a journey through emotions, and an ode to the human experience. Its impact on the literary world reverberates with significance, earning it the acclaim and reverence it rightfully deserves. For lovers of poetry seeking depth, beauty, and introspection, "Exits" stands as a magnificent and enriching work that beckons to be explored and cherished.

ABOUT POLLOCK

Stephen Pollock is a polymath whose life has been a woven with threads of poetry, medicine, and innovation. His journey into the realm of poetry began in childhood, where the cardboard from his father's Oxford shirts served as the canvas for his earliest poetic expressions. This affinity for verse matured during his time at Amherst College, culminating in a fervent five-week endeavor to compose a metaphysical poem, emblematic of his passion for the interplay between subjective and objective reality.

Despite his deep-seated connection with poetry, Pollock embarked on a distinguished career in medicine, specializing in neuro-ophthalmology. At Duke University, he served as Chief of Neuro-Ophthalmology, where he not only provided clinical care but also contributed significantly to the field through research and mentorship. His expertise led him to publish numerous papers in the medical literature, establishing himself as a leading figure in his field.

However, Pollock's professional journey took an unexpected turn when he transitioned to the realm of business, becoming the chief executive of CEC (Community Eye Care). Under his leadership, CEC flourished, offering voluntary vision benefits to employees through their employers. Despite officially retiring from CEC in 2017, Pollock remained instrumental in overseeing the company's sale for the subsequent two years.

Beyond medicine and business, Pollock's curiosity and ingenuity extended into the domains of engineering and technology. His collaboration during medical school resulted in the development of a groundbreaking variable-focus lens, leading to the granting of a U.S. patent. Additionally, his inventions have facilitated the biopsy of previously inaccessible tumors within the orbit and brain, showcasing his multidisciplinary approach to problem-solving.

Stephen Pollock's life embodies the synergy of diverse passions and pursuits, where poetry, medicine, entrepreneurship, and innovation converge to form a rich tapestry of achievement.

THE RISKS OF DIY DENTISTRY

Why Some Things Are Best Left to Professionals

"DIY dentistry poses risks like irreversible damage and overlooked issues. ADA warns against at-home treatments, emphasizing personalized care from dentists for safe, effective solutions and long-term oral health."

PHOTO BY NENSURIA / ISTOCK VIA GETTY IMAGES PLUS

DIY activities, like swapping a lighting fixture or painting your living room, are popular ways to accomplish your to-do list. But as anyone who has tackled too big of a project knows, some jobs are best left to the professionals. That includes your dental health.

You may have already seen DIY dentistry products, such as at-home whitening kits, mouthguards or teeth aligners. These often guarantee fast, easy ways to solve your oral health issues without the involvement of a dentist or an orthodontist (a dentist who specializes in the bite and alignment of your teeth).

"Dental products are never one-size-fits-all," said American Dental Association (ADA) president, Linda Edgar, D.D.S. "No two mouths are alike, which is why it's important to work directly with an ADA dentist or orthodontist to determine the precise care that your body needs."

Skipping the dentist chair and "fixing" your teeth at home can lead to bigger, sometimes irreversible problems. For some people with more complex dental health needs, using an at-home aligner may cause bone loss, lost teeth, receding gums, bite problems, jaw pain and other damaging and permanent issues. You might also not be aware of other dental issues that should be addressed before you start moving teeth.

"Patients are understandably drawn to these DIY treatments because they might struggle to fit a dentist appointment into their schedule or they assume at-home care will cost less," Dr. Edgar said. "But when these products cause major issues, patients end up spending more

"Don't gamble with your oral health. Consult a dentist for safe, effective treatment."

time and more money trying to reverse that damage. Instead, trained ADA dentists and orthodontists can talk through patients' budget concerns and offer them a wider variety of dependable, approved treatment options."

In between dental checkups, look for products with the ADA Seal of Acceptance. These have been independently evaluated by experts and recognized to be both safe and effective. When you choose one of these options, you can be assured that your care is backed by evidence-based research and generations of scientific knowledge.

Whether it's teeth grinding or a toothache, talk to your dentist before trying to solve your dental problems on your own. A dentist can help you find a personalized treatment plan that's

right for you, monitor your progress and make recommendations on how to manage your oral health outside of the office.

To look for an ADA dentist in your area, visit findadentist.ada.org.

"The ADA's primary concerns with DIY dentistry are, and always have been, patient safety and quality care," Dr. Edgar said. "Our job as dentists is to put patient health first." (STATE POINT)

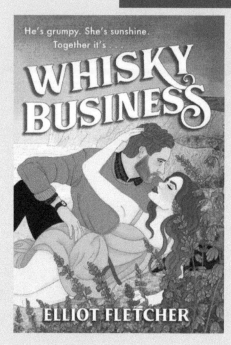

THE MUMPRENEUR DIARIES

By Mosey Jones

Business, Babies or Bust - One Mother of a Year

Business, Babies or Bust - One Mother of a YearThe Mumpreneur Diaries by Mosey Jones offers a refreshingly honest portrayal of the highs and lows of juggling motherhood and entrepreneurship. Jones' journey from the confines of a corporate commute to the unpredictable world of working from home with two young boys is both relatable and entertaining.

Jones' decision to embark on her mumpreneurial venture is sparked by a moment of clarity during her pregnant commute, where the allure of flexible hours and more time with her children becomes irresistible. However, as she delves into the world of running her own business while managing her family, she quickly discovers that the path to success is riddled with challenges.

From sleepless nights to financial crises and marital strains, Jones candidly shares the struggles that accompany the pursuit of her entrepreneurial dreams. Yet, amidst the chaos, her narrative is infused with humor and warmth, making it a delightful read.

The Mumpreneur Diaries serves as both a cautionary tale and an inspiration for aspiring mumpreneurs, offering valuable insights into the realities of balancing motherhood and entrepreneurship. Jones' down-to-earth approach and witty storytelling make this 'mumoir' a captivating and motivating read for anyone considering taking the leap into entrepreneurship while raising a family.

WHISKY BUSINESS

By Elliot Fletcher

"One flirty Hollywood actress. One grumpy Scottish islander. One magnetic connection."

Whisky Business by Elliot Fletcher delivers a delightful blend of romance, humor, and whisky-soaked charm in the picturesque setting of the Isle of Skye. April Sinclair, a fallen Hollywood star, finds herself back in her Scottish hometown, determined to revive her family's whisky distillery. Little does she expect to clash with the ruggedly handsome and irritable master distiller, Malcolm Macabe.

Fletcher crafts a compelling enemies-to-lovers narrative, weaving together April and Mal's fiery chemistry with the backdrop of whisky-making traditions. Mal's gruff demeanor and April's glamorous persona create a dynamic tension that keeps the pages turning.

The Isle of Skye provides a stunning backdrop for the story, immersing readers in its rugged beauty and atmospheric charm. Fletcher's vivid descriptions bring the setting to life, evoking a sense of place that adds depth to the narrative.

But it's not just the setting that shines in "Whisky Business." The steamy romance between April and Mal adds a sizzling tension to the story, keeping readers hooked until the very end.

Whisky Business is a captivating romcom that balances humor, heart, and heat in equal measure. Fletcher's witty prose and irresistible characters make this a must-read for fans of enemies-to-lovers romance.

BUY, BUY BABY

by Susan Gregory Thomas

"The book captivates with its blend of romance and intrigue, showcasing Herkness's masterful storytelling prowess. A must-read!"

Buy Buy Baby by Susan Gregory Thomas offers a compelling exposé on the insidious tactics employed by multinational corporations to target infants and toddlers as consumers. Drawing parallels to seminal works like "No Logo" and "Fast Food Nation," Thomas unveils the unsettling reality of how big business manipulates parental anxieties and exploits child development research to peddle products to the youngest demographic.

With meticulous research, Thomas delves into the marketing strategies that saturate the market with seemingly educational toys and media, masking profit-driven agendas. She adeptly navigates through the landscape of brands like Disney, McDonald's, and Barbie, revealing their pervasive influence on young minds.

As a parent and seasoned journalist, Thomas brings a unique perspective to the discussion, underscoring the detrimental effects of consumerism on early childhood development. Her insights shed light on the alarming rise of anxiety and hyper-competitiveness among children, echoing the concerns of many contemporary parents.

Buy Buy Baby is not just a critique of corporate practices; it's a call to action against the commodification of childhood. Thomas's work serves as a timely reminder of the ethical implications of marketing to vulnerable demographics and underscores the urgent need for conscientious consumption.

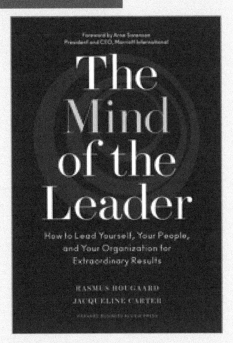

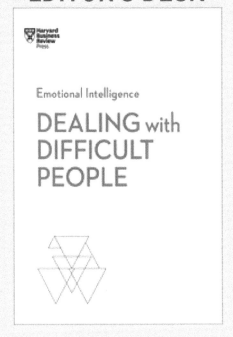

PLAYING TO WIN

by A.G. Lafley and Roger Martin

"Essential playbook for strategic success. Lafley and Martin offer practical wisdom that transforms businesses. A must-read for aspiring leaders."

Playing to Win: How Strategy Really Works by A.G. Lafley and Roger Martin is a must-read for anyone looking to understand the essence of successful business strategy. Drawing from his extensive experience as CEO of Procter & Gamble, Lafley, along with strategic adviser Roger Martin, provides a comprehensive guidebook for navigating the complexities of modern business.

Through compelling narratives and insightful analysis, Lafley and Martin unveil the strategic approach that propelled P&G to unprecedented success during Lafley's tenure. By focusing on essential elements such as where to play and how to win, the authors demonstrate how leaders can align everyday actions with overarching strategic goals to achieve remarkable results.

The book is not merely a theoretical exposition; it is a practical playbook filled with real-world examples of how P&G transformed iconic brands like Olay, Gillette, and Swiffer into market leaders through strategic decision-making. Lafley's return to P&G underscores the enduring relevance of the strategies outlined in this book, making it essential reading for executives, entrepreneurs, and anyone seeking to gain a competitive edge in today's dynamic business landscape.

Playing to Win is a compelling blend of theory and practice, offering invaluable insights that will undoubtedly resonate with readers striving not just to play the game, but to emerge victorious.

THE MIND OF THE LEADER

by Rasmus Hougaard and Jacqueline Carter

"The Mind of the Leader offers a transformative approach, advocating mindfulness, selflessness, and compassion, providing actionable strategies for effective leadership.

The Mind of the Leader: How to Lead Yourself, Your People, and Your Organization for Extraordinary Results by Rasmus Hougaard and Jacqueline Carter presents a compelling argument for a fundamental shift in leadership philosophy. Backed by comprehensive research and insightful interviews, the book sheds light on a pressing global issue: the disconnect between leaders and their teams.

Hougaard and Carter paint a stark picture of the current leadership landscape, where despite significant investments in development, employees feel disengaged and undervalued. Through their exploration of the basic human needs of meaning, purpose, connection, and happiness in the workplace, they pinpoint the root of this disengagement.

What sets "The Mind of the Leader" apart is its pragmatic approach to tackling the leadership crisis. By advocating for mindfulness, selflessness, and compassion as core mental qualities for effective leadership, the authors offer a refreshing perspective. Drawing on real-world examples from top organizations, they demonstrate how embracing these qualities can lead to transformative results.

This book is not just a critique of existing leadership paradigms; it's a roadmap for change. It challenges leaders to prioritize people over profits and provides actionable strategies for doing so. *The Mind of the Leader* is a must-read for anyone invested in fostering a more inclusive, compassionate, and ultimately successful organizational culture.

DEALING WITH DIFFICULT PEOPLE

by Harvard Business Review, Tony Schwartz, Mark Gerzon, Holly Weeks, Amy Gallo

"Insightful and practical advice from expert contributors. Essential reading for mastering workplace dynamics and fostering productive relationships effectively."

Dealing with Difficult People is a comprehensive guide to navigating the challenging dynamics often encountered in professional environments. Authored by a team of experts including Tony Schwartz, Mark Gerzon, Holly Weeks, and Amy Gallo, the book delves into the intricate interplay of emotions that characterize interactions with troublesome colleagues.

Central to its message is the importance of managing emotions, both one's own and those of others, in order to foster more productive relationships. Through a blend of research-backed insights and practical advice, the book equips readers with the tools to remain composed during tough conversations and to effectively address passive-aggressive behavior.

Part of the acclaimed HBR Emotional Intelligence Series, this book offers essential reading for anyone seeking to enhance their interpersonal skills in the workplace. It not only provides strategies for managing difficult individuals but also encourages self-reflection to recognize one's own contributions to workplace dynamics.

With contributions from renowned thought leaders in the field, *Dealing with Difficult People* is a valuable resource for ambitious professionals looking to cultivate empathy, resilience, and emotional intelligence in their pursuit of success. Uplifting and practical, it offers actionable insights that are indispensable for navigating the complexities of professional relationships.

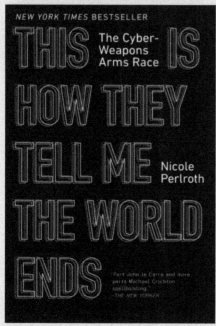

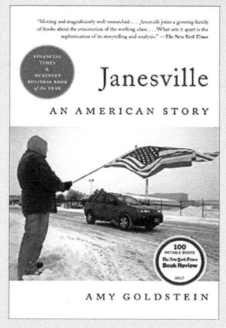

THIS IS HOW THEY TELL ME THE WORLD ENDS

by Nicole Perlroth

> *"Nicole Perlroth's "This Is How They Tell Me the World Ends" is nothing short of a masterpiece in investigative journalism."*

Nicole Perlroth's *This Is How They Tell Me the World Ends* is a chilling exposé delving into the clandestine realm of cyberweapons, unearthing a world veiled in secrecy yet wielding immense power over global security. Through meticulous research and riveting storytelling, Perlroth sheds light on the elusive market of zero-day exploits, the prized tools capable of infiltrating and manipulating critical systems with unprecedented stealth.

With the United States as its focal point, Perlroth unveils the unsettling reality of how governments amassed and exploited zero-days for decades, only to lose control, thereby unleashing a perilous arms race. The narrative brims with a diverse cast, from government agents to hackers, illuminating their intricate dance within this shadowy market. Against the backdrop of escalating cyber threats, Perlroth skillfully weaves together the high-stakes drama with insightful analysis, highlighting the grave implications for global security.

This Is How They Tell Me the World Ends not only captivates with its thriller-like narrative but also serves as a vital wake-up call. Perlroth's blend of investigative journalism and expert commentary delivers a sobering account of the urgent need to address the escalating cyber arms race. As the world grapples with mounting cyber threats, Perlroth's work stands as a compelling testament to the imperative of vigilance and cooperation in safeguarding against digital vulnerabilities. Engrossing and enlightening, this book is an essential read for anyone concerned about the future of global security in the digital age.

JANESVILLE

Amy Goldstein

> *"Service's Lines in the Sand is a poignant masterpiece, weaving raw emotion and introspection into an unforgettable journey of self-discovery."*

Janesville by Amy Goldstein is a compelling narrative that transcends the boundaries of a single town to offer a profound reflection on the broader socio-economic landscape of America. Set against the backdrop of Janesville, Wisconsin, Goldstein meticulously chronicles the aftermath of the closure of its General Motors assembly plant during the Great Recession. Unlike other accounts that focus solely on the immediate shock of job loss, Goldstein delves deep into the lives of its residents, revealing the long-term repercussions on individuals, families, and the community. Through her immersive storytelling, she portrays the resilience and resourcefulness of Janesville's inhabitants as they confront the harsh realities of economic upheaval.

One of the book's strengths lies in its diverse array of voices, capturing the perspectives of autoworkers, educators, politicians, bankers, and job re-trainers. Goldstein skillfully navigates the intersection of economics and politics, shedding light on the complex dynamics shaping contemporary America. *Janesville* is not just a local story—it is an American story that confronts readers with uncomfortable truths about the fragility of the social safety net and the daunting obstacles facing the working class. In conclusion, "Janesville" stands as a testament to the resilience of the human spirit in the face of adversity, offering a narrative of hope, perseverance, and the will to forge a brighter future against all odds.

THE EVERYTHING STORE

by Brad Stone

In "The Everything Store," Brad Stone delves deep into the enigmatic world of Amazon and its pioneering founder, Jeff Bezos. From its humble beginnings as an online bookstore to its evolution into the global powerhouse it is today, Stone unveils the relentless ambition and visionary leadership that propelled Amazon to become "the everything store."

Stone paints a vivid portrait of Bezos, a man driven by an insatiable hunger for innovation and expansion. Bezos's unwavering determination to redefine retail led Amazon into uncharted territory, from the development of the Kindle to its groundbreaking ventures in cloud computing. Through meticulous research and compelling narrative, Stone illustrates how Bezos's bold decisions reshaped not only the retail landscape but also the very fabric of the internet itself.

What sets "The Everything Store" apart is its exploration of Amazon's corporate culture, characterized by an aura of secrecy and a relentless pursuit of excellence. Stone offers readers a glimpse into the inner workings of a company known for its unconventional practices and its relentless focus on customer satisfaction. By uncovering the mechanisms behind Amazon's success, Stone sheds light on the intricate balance between innovation and disruption that defines the company's ethos.

One of the most captivating aspects of Stone's narrative is his portrayal of Amazon's pivotal role in shaping the digital age. By placing one of the earliest and largest bets on the internet, Amazon not only transformed the way we shop but also paved the way for a new era of technological innovation. Through gripping storytelling and insightful analysis, Stone chronicles Amazon's journey from a fledgling startup to a titan of industry, leaving an indelible mark on the world in its wake.

In conclusion, "The Everything Store" is a captivating exploration of Amazon's rise to prominence and the visionary leadership of Jeff Bezos. Through Stone's masterful storytelling, readers are offered a front-row seat to witness the birth of a revolution in retail and technology. Whether you're an entrepreneur, a business enthusiast, or simply curious about the inner workings of one of the world's most influential companies, this book is a must-read. Stone's meticulous research and engaging prose make "The Everything Store" an essential addition to any library, offering invaluable insights into the past, present, and future of commerce in the digital age.

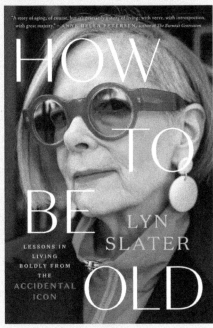

NAOMI OSAKA

By Ben Rothenberg

"Rothenberg's biography of Naomi Osaka illuminates her inspiring journey, capturing her impact on tennis, social justice, and mental health."

In *Naomi Osaka: Her Journey to Finding Her Power and Her Voice*, Ben Rothenberg delves deep into the life of the tennis sensation, uncovering the captivating narrative behind her rise to prominence. Rothenberg adeptly navigates through Osaka's meteoric ascent in the tennis world, from her headline-making victory over Serena Williams at the 2018 US Open to her subsequent triumphs on the Grand Slam stage.

What sets Rothenberg's biography apart is its focus not just on Osaka's on-court achievements but also on her off-court impact. Through meticulous research and compelling storytelling, Rothenberg sheds light on Osaka's journey as an advocate for racial justice and mental health, showcasing her as a trailblazer who transcends the boundaries of sports.

The biography also offers invaluable insights into Osaka's personal background, notably her Haitian-Japanese-American heritage and her family's unwavering support throughout her career. By unraveling the intricacies of Osaka's upbringing and her quest to navigate the complexities of fame and identity, Rothenberg paints a vivid portrait of a remarkable individual.

Naomi Osaka is a must-read for tennis aficionados and casual fans alike, offering a comprehensive exploration of one of the most influential figures in sports today. Rothenberg's narrative skillfully captures the essence of Osaka's resilience, determination, and unwavering commitment to making a difference both on and off the court.

NOT YOUR CHINA DOLL

By Katie Gee Salisbury

"Rothenberg's 'Not Your China Doll' captivates with vivid storytelling, celebrating Anna May Wong's groundbreaking journey in Hollywood."

Not Your China Doll by Ben Rothenberg delves into the captivating journey of Anna May Wong, the trailblazing Asian American movie star of Hollywood's golden era. Rothenberg skillfully navigates Wong's ascent from humble beginnings in Los Angeles to international stardom, shedding light on her struggles against typecasting and racial stereotypes in the film industry.

Set against the glitz and glamor of 1920s Los Angeles, Rothenberg paints a vivid portrait of Wong as a legendary beauty and fashion icon who defied societal expectations. Through meticulous research and engaging prose, he chronicles her rise to fame in Douglas Fairbanks's The Thief of Bagdad and her subsequent rebellion against Hollywood's discriminatory practices.

Wong's bold decision to challenge Hollywood's racism by seeking opportunities abroad is portrayed with poignancy and admiration. Rothenberg masterfully captures the essence of Wong's audacity and resilience as she navigates through a world of capricious directors, glamorous parties, and far-flung love affairs.

Not Your China Doll is a compelling tribute to a pioneering artist who paved the way for future generations of Asian American actors. Rothenberg's debut book is a must-read for anyone interested in cinema history and the ongoing struggle for representation in the entertainment industry.

HOW TO BE OLD

By Lyn Slater

"How to Be Old" by Lyn Slater empowers readers to embrace aging boldly, redefine beauty standards, and live life on their terms.

How to Be Old by Lyn Slater, also known as the "Accidental Icon," is a refreshing and empowering memoir that challenges societal norms surrounding aging. Through her personal journey documented over a decade, Slater proves that age is merely a number and should not limit one's ability to live boldly and authentically.

Slater's candid storytelling and unapologetic embrace of her gray hair and wrinkles serve as an inspiration for readers of all ages. She rejects the notion of fading into the background as one grows older and instead encourages readers to redefine their perceptions of aging. Her message resonates deeply, emphasizing the importance of self-acceptance and embracing change with optimism and creativity.

With wit and wisdom, Slater demonstrates that the process of reinvention knows no bounds. She encourages readers to challenge societal standards of beauty and youth, advocating for a more inclusive and empowering definition of successful aging. Through her narrative, Slater showcases the potential for growth, connection, and creativity in every stage of life.

How to Be Old is not just a memoir; it's a manifesto for living life on one's own terms. Slater's fearless approach to aging serves as a beacon of hope and empowerment for readers seeking to navigate the complexities of getting older. This paradigm-shifting book is a must-read for anyone looking to embrace the fullness of life at any age.

Navigating the Future Dr. Terry McIvor's Vision for PNLPsy™ and Mental Health Support

"Dr. Terry Mcivor, founder of IGH3P®, pioneers PNLPsy™, integrating NLP, psychology, and neuroscience. Empirical validation and ethical integrity define his approach, shaping the future of coaching and mental health support globally."

We had the privilege of interviewing with pioneering psychologist Dr. Terry McIvor, President and Founder of the International Guild of Hypnotherapy, NLP, and 3 Principles Practitioners and Trainers (IGH3P®), to discuss his ground-breaking work in Pathophysiological Neuro Linguistic Psychology (PNLPsy™).

As an academic leader with expertise spanning neuroscience, psychiatric psychology, and empirical research, Dr. McIvor has dedicated his career to advancing the psychological sciences. Through his innovative integration of neuro-linguistic programming, empirical psychology, and neuroscience, Dr. McIvor is spearheading the development of PNLPsy™ - a revolutionary new framework poised to transform coaching, mentoring, and psychological therapies.

In this exclusive interview, Dr. McIvor shares with us the genesis of PNLPsy™, its immense potential to address pressing psychological needs, and his unwavering commitment to evidence-based practices and ethical integrity. We gain powerful insights into how PNLPsy™ leverages neuroplasticity for psychological change, sets new benchmarks for efficacy in coaching/mentoring, and promises to shape the future of psychological disciplines globally.

From his collaboration with elite specialists to his role leading IGH3P® in standardizing industry practices, it is clear this psychologist-turned-trailblazing-entrepreneur has set his sights on no less than a paradigm shift in his field. The implications of his pioneering work in PNLPsy™ cannot be overstated.

Can you share the inspiration behind creating Pathophysiological Neuro Linguistic Psychology (PNLPsy™) and what led you to combine Neuro-Linguistic Programming (NLP), empirical psychology, and neuroscience in this innovative field?

The development and continuing development of PNLPsy™ was and is quite a personal journey for me. As Chair of Psychology at Manipur International University, I've been in a unique position to observe the overlap and, sometimes, the gaps between various psychological disciplines. The idea was to create a discipline that not only bridges these gaps but also stands up to the rigours of empirical testing. With the university's resources, I'm excited about the prospect of conducting clinical trials to validate the efficacy of PNLPsy™ techniques.

How do you envision PNLPsy™ contributing to the evolution of psychological sciences, and what unique advantages does it offer over traditional approaches?

PNLPsy™ is set to make a significant mark on the psychological sciences. With the ability to conduct clinical trials at the university, we're not just theorising; we're proving. This evidence-based approach, combined with the practical aspects of NLP and the insights from neuroscience, offers a comprehensive framework that I believe will revolutionise how we understand and apply psychological practices.

As the CEO of the International Guild of Hypnotherapy, NLP, and 3 Principles Practitioners and Trainers, how do you see PNLPsy™ influencing coaching and mentoring standards within the professional community?

Leading the International Guild of Hypnotherapy, NLP, and 3 Principles Practitioners and Trainers has connected me with an extensive network of professionals. As we develop PNLPsy™, this network becomes invaluable, allowing us to set new benchmarks in coaching and mentoring. We're not just teaching; we're rigorously testing our methodologies to ensure they meet the highest standards of efficacy and ethics. While also working with the coaching and mentoring regulator.

In your opinion, how does the integrative approach of PNLPsy™ enhance the effectiveness of psychological interventions, and what potential impact could it have on addressing psychological issues?

The integrative approach of PNLPsy™, underpinned by solid research and clinical trials, naturally enhances the effectiveness of psychological interventions. We're not guessing here; we're applying scientifically validated techniques tailored to individual needs, ensuring our interventions are as impactful as possible.

Could you provide examples of therapeutic approaches within PNLPsy™ that leverage neuroplasticity to address psychological challenges?

At the heart of PNLPsy™ is

Dr. Terry Mcivor, President and Founder of IGH3P®, leading the charge in revolutionizing psychological sciences with the innovative NLPsy™ approach"

our focus on neuroplasticity, and being in a leadership position in a university department allows me to explore this through clinical research. We're developing therapeutic approaches that harness the brain's ability to rewire itself, offering hope and tangible results for those facing psychological challenges. The integration of sound psychological neurology and a sophisticated understanding of neuroplasticity into PNLPsy™ not only distinguishes it from traditional NLP but also ensures that it remains a dynamic, scientifically grounded discipline. As we continue to explore the complexity of the human brain, PNLPsy™ stands ready to adapt and incorporate these discoveries, promising a future of psychological practice that is both effective and deeply rooted in neuroscience.

How does PNLPsy™ address the issue of pseudoscience in psychology, and what steps are taken to ensure that its methodologies are firmly grounded in evidence-based practices?

One of my key missions with PNLPsy™ is to clear the fog of pseudoscience that can sometimes cloud our field. Through rigorous clinical trials and a commitment to empirical evidence, we will ensure that PNLPsy™ stands as an example of a scientifically validated practice in psychology. We want to standardise the coaching industry, increasing standards and weeding out the cowboys and cowgirls.

In terms of professional development, how does PNLPsy™ support coaches and mentors in accessing scientifically validated tools and techniques for their practice?

With the establishment of my accredited international professional body, IGH3P®, we're in a prime position to support coaches and mentors with tools and techniques that aren't just effective but are proven to be so. This is about elevating psychology, coaching, and mentoring practices to new heights, backed by solid research and ethical integrity.

Ethics play a crucial role in PNLPsy™. Can you elaborate on the ethical principles guiding this discipline and how they contribute to maintaining integrity in psychological interventions?

Ethics are non-negotiable in PNLPsy™. As we advance this discipline, every step is taken with a deep sense of responsibility towards the individuals we serve. Our ethical guidelines are stringent, ensuring that every aspect of PNLPsy™, from research to practice, upholds the highest standards of integrity.

As a leader in the field, how do you see PNLPsy™ shaping the future of coaching, mentoring, and psychological practices globally?:

With the resources and network at my disposal, I see PNLPsy™ as a pivotal force in shaping the future of psychological practices. We're not just creating a new discipline; we're setting a new standard that insists on empirical validation, ethical practice, and real-world efficacy.

Can you share insights into your collaborative efforts with other well-being professional bodies and how these collaborations contribute to the ongoing development of PNLPsy™?

The development of PNLPsy™ is a collaborative endeavour. Working with a network of professional coaching, research, and accrediting organisations, we're not only advancing PNLPsy™ but also rigorously testing its therapeutic power. This collaborative approach ensures that PNLPsy™ is continually refined, validated, and aligned with the needs of those we aim to serve.

A Tapestry of Colours and Textures Promoting Greek Magic Worldwide

OLIA Scarves, founded by Olympia Theofanopoulou, combines Greek heritage with modern design, sourcing silk from Soufli. Meticulously crafted, each piece reflects Greece's essence, aiming for global recognition.

BY A.J. LONDON SOMER

In the bustling heart of Athens lies a brand that seamlessly blends the essence of art, tradition, and luxury into exquisite wearable pieces. OLIA Scarves, founded by Olympia Theofanopoulou, stands as a testament to the rich tapestry of Greek culture and heritage, woven intricately into each silk scarf and pareo. As we delve into the story behind OLIA Scarves, we uncover a journey marked by passion, innovation, and a deep-rooted commitment to craftsmanship.

At the core of OLIA Scarves lies the vision to transform art into wearable masterpieces. Inspired by her love for photography and a chance encounter with locally produced silk in Northern Greece, Olympia embarked on a quest to marry her artistic pursuits with the timeless allure of silk fabric. What began as a spark of inspiration during a visit to the historic town of Soufli evolved into a flourishing venture that celebrates Greece's artistic legacy while embracing modern design aesthetics.

Olympia's background in Archaeological Conservation and Museum Studies, acquired at London's prestigious Institute of Archaeology, served as the foundation for her venture into the world of luxury fashion. With a keen eye for detail honed through years of studying and preserving artworks from around the globe, she brings a unique perspective to the design process at OLIA Scarves. Each piece is meticulously crafted to capture the spontaneity and authenticity of her art photographs, ensuring that every scarf or pareo tells a story of its own.

Sourcing the purest silk from Soufli, a town steeped in silk-producing traditions dating back to Byzantine times, OLIA Scarves pays homage to Greece's rich heritage. The synergy between locally sourced silk and contemporary artistry not only elevates the quality of the products but also fosters sustainable practices within the European silk industry. By promoting two of Soufli's finest silk qualities, Crepe de Chine and Crepe Satin, OLIA Scarves stands as a beacon of ethical fashion, championing the revival of traditional craftsmanship.

As OLIA Scarves sets its sights on the global stage, aspirations of collaboration and innovation loom large on the horizon. With a successful debut at the Pure London & JATC Event, the brand garnered international acclaim, paving the way for future collaborations with artists and companies worldwide. Through its kaleidoscopic array of colours and textures, OLIA Scarves aims to transport a piece of Greece's magic to every corner of the globe, encapsulating the essence of its islands, seascapes, and cultural heritage.

Join us as we embark on a journey through the world of OLIA Scarves, where art becomes adornment, tradition meets

ADORNED IN ELEGANCE:: *Models showcase OLIA Scarves, each a masterpiece fusing art and tradition. From Greece's rich heritage to modern design, these scarves captivate with every fold.*

PHOTOS BY KATERINA CHEILADAKI

Olympia Theofanopoulou, a visionary blending heritage with innovation, epitomizes artistry and dedication. Through OLIA Scarves, her passion illuminates, weaving tales of Greek culture and luxury with impeccable craftsmanship.

innovation, and luxury finds its truest expression in the embrace of Greek silk.

What inspired the creation of OLIA Scarves?

The founder, Olympia Theofanopoulou, was inspired during a visit to Soufli in Northern Greece, where she encountered locally produced silk. Impressed by its quality, she envisioned combining her art photographs with this luxurious material.

How did Olympia Theofanopoulou's background influence the founding of OLIA Scarves?

- Olympia studied Archaeological Conservation and Museum Studies in London, which provided her with opportunities to visit art galleries and museums worldwide. Her studies and profession in conservation, coupled with her passion for photography, influenced her attention to detail and the unique design of OLIA Scarves.

Where does OLIA Scarves source its silk from, and what is its significance?

OLIA Scarves sources its silk from Soufli, a small town in Northeastern Greece known for its historical significance in silk production. Soufli's climate and silk-producing traditions contrib-

ute to the superior quality of the silk, which is attributed to the silkworms feeding on sykamore tree leaves.

What is the process involved in creating a silk scarf or pareo at OLIA Scarves?

The process involves several stages, including photograph selection, processing, colour testing, digital printing, fixing, drying, cutting, and finishing. Attention to detail ensures that each item combines the artistic elements of the photographs with the unique qualities of Greek silk.

What are OLIA Scarves' future aspirations and collaboration plans?

OLIA Scarves aims to showcase Greece's cultural heritage and natural beauty through its products, with aspirations to expand globally and collaborate with artists and companies worldwide. Their scarves feature details and fragments of the Greek landscape, capturing small miracles often overlooked.

Can you describe OLIA Scarves' experience at the Pure London & JATC Event?

The Pure London & JATC Event provided OLIA Scarves with their first exposure to the

international market, offering invaluable insights and attracting visitors from various countries. The experience was enhanced by the publication of an article in the UK Entrepreneur Prime Magazine.

How does OLIA Scarves maintain its focus on quality and authenticity?

OLIA Scarves ensures that its photographs convey spontaneity and authenticity, avoiding stylization. Attention to detail extends beyond technique to combine artistic elements with the unique qualities of Greek silk, resulting in luxury items that bestow beauty and elegance.

What role does photography play in the creation of OLIA Scarves?

Photography is a fundamental aspect of OLIA Scarves, with founder Olympia Theofanopoulou's passion for art photography driving the brand's creation. The photographs, mainly drawn from Greece's rich history and natural treasures, are transformed into wearable luxury items, adding an intangible, ethereal essence to the scarves.

SIMONA SPAN'S
STORMY NIGHT

"Embrace your uniqueness and step into the spotlight with Simona Span's signature 'Stormy Night' dress, where elegance meets empowerment. Join the journey of resilience and creativity, inspired by Romanian heritage, as passion becomes purpose."

Simona Span's Journey to Global Fashion Stardom

Empowering Women, Embracing Sustainability, and Redefining Style, One Stitch at a Timevolor sim expe conseque

Simona Span, founder of Simona Span Fashion, shares her journey from creating for her daughters to international acclaim. Her designs embrace sustainability, empower women, and envision innovative collaborations.

In the heart of Romania, amidst the serene landscapes of Negresti Oas, Simona Șpan, a proud mother of four, found her sanctuary and her calling. Her story is one of resilience, creativity, and an unwavering commitment to her dreams. From the quaint charm of her small town upbringing to the bustling runways of international fashion events, Simona's journey is nothing short of remarkable.

Amidst the challenges of the pandemic, Simona sought solace in the art of dressmaking, initially crafting garments for her daughters. Little did she know that this therapeutic endeavour would blossom into a flourishing fashion label, captivating hearts far beyond her hometown. Simona's creations, infused with love and inspired by her Romanian heritage, soon caught the eye of fashion enthusiasts worldwide.

In our exclusive interview with Simona Șpan for Entrepreneur Prime magazine, we delve into the intricacies of her ascent from a home-based hobbyist to a celebrated designer with a global presence. Her transition from sewing for her daughters to establishing her own fashion empire underscores the transformative power of passion and perseverance.

Simona's designs not only reflect her personal narrative but also resonate deeply with her clientele, embodying the spirit of empowerment and individuality. Her recent experience at the Pure London x JATC exhibition opened doors to new horizons, propelling her towards collaborations that bridge the worlds of fashion, art, and entertainment.

As sustainability takes centre stage in the fashion industry, Simona Șpan remains committed to ethical production practices. Her timeless creations, devoid of fleeting trends, embrace sustainability by prioritizing small-scale production and resource efficiency.

With each unique dress she creates, Simona Șpan champions the ethos of self-love and confidence, encouraging women to embrace their uniqueness with pride. Looking ahead, she envisions a future where technology and design converge to drive innovation while preserving precious resources.

Join us as we embark on a journey through Simona Șpan's world of fashion, where passion meets purpose, and dreams know no bounds.

What inspired you to transition from creating dresses for your daughters to establishing your own fashion label?

My biggest inspiration for expanding my brand, was the happiness of my clients. Whenever I was creating a dress for someone, the excitement in their eyes and the pure joy of wearing my designs, kept me going and motivated me to create more and more.

How do you believe your personal story and the beginnings of your brand resonate with your clientele?

I think lots of women out there resonate with my story. A single mother, trying her best, pushing the boundries, getting out of her confort zone just to be able to provide a good future for her daughters and following her passion! I would love to know that I'm a source of inspiration for women and show them that nothing is impossible and is never too late to follow your dream!

Could you share with us a highlight from your recent experience at the Pure London x JATC exhibition?

I had no idea what to expect from Pure London x JATC, but many people, after seeing my dresses on the catwalk, came to me and encouraged me to expand my work and my vision towards movie, cinema and theatre world, combining my work with art like opera, exhibitions of painting and other exclusivist events.

How does your Romanian heritage influence your designs, and how are you integrating this into the global fashion scene?

My designs are influenced by the places I've grew up in. I love colours, I love nature, the floral prints, the landscapes from my hometown were my biggest source of inspiration.

What challenges have you faced in scaling your brand from a local business to an international one, and how have you overcome them?

Actually I cannot talk about a local business, because after my first appereance in Romania, almost every invitation that followed was international: Italy, Canada, Dubai, France, England, America. In some we were able to go, but some of them are on our pending list, looking forward to go this year.

Sustainability is a significant conversation in fashion today. How does Simona Șpan address sustainability in its production processes?

Thanks to the fact that our dresses are timeless, so they don't follow trends, sustainability inside our company translates into limiting production to small series, without unnecessary merchandise stocks and avoiding the consumption of resources until they are clearly dedicated to a targeted consumption.

What is the philosophy behind the unique dresses you create, and how do you want women to feel when wearing your designs?

The philosophy behind my designs is that every woman is unique and special. Every woman should embrace this uniqueness and love everything about her, feel empowered, have confidence and be brave enough to wear something that is created just for her!

Looking towards the future, what direction do you see Simona Șpan taking, and are there any upcoming projects or collaborations we can look forward to?

Now we work at a new project that will combine new technology with design, specially developed to save resources such as fabrics, time, production costs. This project comes to help the production efficiency and implementing sustainability too.

How
Heidi Ellert-McDermott
Transformed Speechwriting with
Innovation, Wit, and SpeechyAI

Heidi Ellert-McDermott's Speechy revolutionizes speechwriting, born from a need for witty wedding speeches. Overcoming SEO challenges, Speechy offers diverse services, led by top-notch writers. Marketing through PR and a book, Speechy aims to expand with SpeechyAI, balancing entrepreneurship with life challenges.

There are those that stand out not just for their innovation, but for their profound impact on personal moments and milestones. Enter Heidi Ellert-McDermott, a visionary entrepreneur who has reshaped the landscape of speechwriting with her brainchild, Speechy.

Heidi's journey into the realm of speechwriting was sparked by a cascade of wedding experiences where the speeches ranged from lackluster to cringe-worthy. Drawing from her background as a TV director and writer at the esteemed BBC, Heidi recognized an unmet need for modern, witty, and bespoke wedding speeches. Thus, Speechy was born.

What sets Speechy apart is not just its impeccable craftsmanship but also its adaptability. Evolving from its roots in wedding speeches, the company now offers a spectrum of services tailored to diverse needs and budgets. From speech edits to delivery coaching and even the groundbreaking SpeechyAI, Heidi's team ensures that every word resonates with authenticity and humor.

But the road to success was not without its challenges. Like any entrepreneur, Heidi faced the daunting task of navigating uncharted territory, from understanding SEO to mastering the art of delegation. Yet, fueled by her unwavering passion and commitment to excellence, she persevered, propelling Speechy to global acclaim.

What truly distinguishes Speechy is the caliber of its team. Comprised of industry luminaries who have graced the stages of BBC comedy shows and penned jokes for renowned comedians, Speechy's writers bring unparalleled expertise and warmth to every project. It's this winning combination of talent and empathy that has earned Speechy accolades from publications like The Observer and The New York Times.

As Heidi looks toward the future, her sights are set on further revolutionising the world of speechwriting with SpeechyAI. Powered by artificial intelligence and honed by the wisdom of Heidi's team, SpeechyAI promises to redefine how we craft speeches for weddings, businesses, and celebrations alike.

In the midst of her entrepreneurial journey, Heidi acknowledges the perpetual quest for balance between work and life, a challenge she tackles with characteristic grace and determination. Yet, through it all, her unwavering dedication to her craft and her clients remains steadfast, ensuring that every speech crafted by Speechy is not just memorable but truly unforgettable.

Join us as we delve into the remarkable story of Heidi Ellert-McDermott and the transformative power of Speechy, where every word is crafted with care and every moment is imbued with laughter and love.

How did you get the idea for your business and why did you think it would work?

In my early 30s I went to a succession of weddings where the speeches were variable to say the least. The brilliant ones added a wonderful moment to the day, but more often than not, the speeches were either awkward or dull. After sitting through a 40 min speech and seeing a trio of best men escorted away from the mic, I realised wedding speakers might appreciate the help for professional speechwriters.

Having worked in the TV industry, I had lots of contacts who I knew could work well with people and create truly unique and witty speeches for them. My team have worked on topical news quizzes and ghostwrite for renowned comedians, so wedding speakers now have access to truly great writers at a reasonable cost.

Over the years, we've developed our offering so in response to our clients varying needs, ability and budgets. We now also offer...

• A speech edit service (where clients send their first draft and we make it better)

• Delivery coaching (having directed TV presenters for over a decade, I know the dos and don't of presenting)

• Speech templates – (cheap, fast

Heidi Ellert-McDermott revolutionises speechwriting with Speechy, offering bespoke, witty speeches. From weddings to celebrations, her team, backed by SpeechyAI, crafts unforgettable moments with innovation and expertise."

turnaround option)

• SpeechyAI (combining our expertise with Artificial Intelligence)

What challenges did you find at the beginning of your journey and how did you overcome them?

Having never run my own business, I was completely ignorant about everything, other than the speechwriting and setting up a strong team!

The biggest learning curve has been understanding SEO as all our business is done online. We are a global business that offers both bespoke services and e-commerce products and we market to a wide variety of demographics (from best men in Australia wanting a bespoke speech, to a mother of the groom in the States wanting a simple speech template) so understanding our keywords and focussing our targeting has been key to our growth.

What makes your business unique?

Without a doubt, the quality of the Speechy team. They really are top of their game; writing for a range of BBC topical comedy shows, appearing in panel shows and ghostwriting for world-renowned comedians. They are also genuinely lovely people to work with and are excellent at building strong relationships with our clients.

What advice would you give to someone who is trying to become an entrepreneur?

It's not easy! Everything takes longer than you hope and costs a lot more too.

There's no silver bullet, and not much downtime in the initial years. There's lots of blood, sweat and tears and running your own business can be tough. But, as long as you know you're providing a great service or product, the effort feels worth it.

At Speechy as offer a delight guarantee because we want all our customers and clients to love working with us. I personally couldn't cope if they didn't! I care too much!

How did you market your business?

Because we offer such an unusual service and we have a lot of expertise, I've found it relatively easy to get good PR. We've been featured everywhere from The Telegraph to Forbes. I've also appeared on Radio 4's Women's Hour and BBC Sounds 'Best Men' podcast.

We don't pay for any editorial features; we simply supply interesting and entertaining content.

Due to our growing reputation as the go-to speech experts, the fantastic Little, Brown Publishers released my book, 'The Modern Couple's Guide to Wedding Speeches' last year. Great how-to book, and great publicity too!

What plans do you have for the future?

Our aim this year is to market SpeechyAI – https://www.speechy.com/product/speechyai/. We're confident it's a game-changer.

SpeechyAI utilises the power of Artificial Intelligence and the Speechy team's expertise to create wedding speeches that are funny, meaningful, and memorable. It's fun to use and affordable.

We'll be constantly improving it as the tech develops and we're also hoping to extend its ability beyond wedding speeches to business and celebration speeches too.

Exciting times ahead!

What's the biggest challenge of being an entrepreneur?

Having a work-life balance. (Still not quite mastered that one!)

Important to be able to delegate.

I've also learnt not to attempt all marketing routes, and instead concentrate on the few that have proven to work for us. It's impossible to master all marketing options – especially with so many social media channels, as well as PPC, mailing lists, SEO, and PR to consider.

Nikki's Path to Conscious Entrepreneurship A Journey of Resilience, Mindfulness, and Sustainable Fashion

Nikki, founder of Conscious Yoga Collective, shares her transformative journey blending mindfulness, sustainability, and fashion. Entrepreneur Prime Magazine explores her story of resilience and purpose-driven entrepreneurship

In the dynamic world of entrepreneurship, stories of resilience, transformation, and purpose-driven ventures often stand out as beacons of inspiration. Nikki, the founder of Conscious Yoga Collective (CYC), embodies precisely such a narrative. From the equestrian world to the realms of mindfulness, sustainability, and fashion, her journey reflects the remarkable fusion of personal passion, social responsibility, and entrepreneurial spirit.

Entrepreneur Prime Magazine had the privilege of sitting down with Nikki to delve into her captivating journey and the evolution of CYC. What began as a quest for divine inspiration

"Nikki's recent foray into the fashion world, marked by a resounding success at the Pure London fashion event, signals a new chapter for CYC.

amidst adversity unfolded into a multifaceted enterprise that not only promotes wellness but also uplifts local communities and champions ethical practices.

Nikki's odyssey from a traumatic hit-and-run incident to embracing mindfulness as a transformative force underscores the power of resilience and adaptability. Drawing from her diverse experiences in yoga, psychology, and sustainable living, she has woven together a brand that transcends conventional boundaries, embracing fashion as a platform for mindfulness and social impact.

India, with its vibrant culture and rich tapestry of traditions, has been instrumental in shaping Nikki's vision. Through CYC, she not only honors her connection to the country but also channels its essence into products that reflect authenticity, craftsmanship, and sustainability.

At the heart of CYC lies a commitment to supporting local artisans and initiatives. Nikki's dedication to fostering partnerships with communities in India not only reflects ethical business practices but also underscores her unwavering belief in the power of collaboration and shared prosperity.

Nikki's recent foray into the fashion world, marked by a resounding success at the Pure London fashion event, signals a new chapter for CYC. As the brand undergoes a rebranding process, retaining its ethical artisan ethos amidst exponential growth, Nikki remains steadfast in her mission to ensure that mindfulness and purpose continue to infuse every facet of the company's journey.

Through this exclusive interview, Entrepreneur Prime Magazine invites readers to delve into the inspiring narrative of Nikki and Conscious Yoga Collective—a testament to the transformative potential of entrepreneurship rooted in mindfulness, sustainability, and social impact

What motivated you to establish Conscious Yoga Collective, and how does the company's mission align with your personal values and aspirations?

I originally founded CYC as a

Nikki, founder of Conscious Yoga Collective (CYC), discussing mindfulness, sustainability, and fashion for a purpose-driven journey with Entrepreneur Prime Magazine.

brand under which I could teach yoga and potentially sell products to supplement my income. I didn't really have a clear direction for what I wanted out of the business or life. Without sounding too naive, I was kind of looking for divine inspiration. I just knew that I wanted to have a business that had the potential to impact lives and communities and would enable me to support people who were dedicating their lives to causes they believe in. That's what I find really inspiring. In terms of my own personal aspirations, I can't say that I have any per se other than support myself through an endeavor where I can feel like I add value, not just to the communities I impact but also with regards to myself; that I feel like I am good at what I do.

Your journey has taken you to India, where you've immersed yourself in its vibrant culture. How has this experience influenced the practices and teachings at Conscious Yoga Collective?

India has played a huge role in my life time and time again. Prior to starting this business, I was visiting my Guru looking for inspiration on what I should consider doing now that I had left my toy company that I had spent roughly 3 years building. I was hoping he would give me a clear picture; however, I remember being incredibly disappointed because he said, "Nikki, you're not going to do one thing. Like a violinist will say I am a violinist, I was born to play the violin. You are not one of those people. You're an entrepreneur; you're going to do many things." I remember feeling so disheartened because I wanted to feel like I had a purpose or a strength. He explained that adaptability was my greatest strength. I only realize now how true that is.

Conscious Yoga Collective places a strong emphasis on supporting local makers and initiatives in India. How do you approach partnerships and collaborations with local communities, and what impact do you hope to achieve through these efforts?

I started making yoga mats out of recycled plastic bottles, and as a side project, I decided to make bags using artisans and sustainable materials. The yoga mats, while sustainable, are not really an artisan product because of the

processes involved in manufacturing, so the bags were supposed to be a cute little social enterprise. They quickly became my full-time business, and now we have 3 factories of local makers working for us. This growth is really exciting for us because we can make a real impact on family businesses and their communities.

You recently attended the Pure London fashion event in London. How does your experience at such events inform the ethos and aesthetic of Conscious Yoga Collective, and do you see any potential intersections between fashion, mindfulness, and wellness in the future of the company?

Definitely. That was my first trade event, and although I had done a lot of consumer events, I didn't anticipate the demand for the products among retailers. In three days, we opened over 100 retail accounts across the UK. The team who run the event explained that they had never seen anything like it in their time in fashion. They are actually now our agents and distributors, as I had to quickly make the decision to get expert help to deal with the volume of orders. I feel like this has all been driven by the retailers and consumers' demands for ethically sourced traceable products that are good quality.

Moving forward, the business is undergoing a bit of a rebrand. It is now becoming purely a fashion brand but maintaining its ethical artisan ethos. I feel that my job will be to ensure that the products are mindfully produced and that as the company grows, we don't lose our emphasis on our people and purpose. It all comes down to the company being adaptable to the changes that it's had to make. That's why we've chosen to continue to use the name CYC, an abbreviated version of our old name, so that we always remember how the brand had to adapt from being a yoga practice to an almost worldwide distributed fashion brand.

Unravelling Urban Dynamics
A Conversation with
Ramon Gras Alomà

"Ramon Gras Alomà, urban visionary and co-founder of Aretian, blends academia and entrepreneurship to reshape urban landscapes. Their groundbreaking methodologies promise transformative impact in sustainable urban design."

In the bustling landscape of urban development, where innovation meets the timeless challenge of sustainable design, one name stands out: Ramon Gras Alomà. An architect of urban futures, Ramon's journey is a testament to the power of interdisciplinary vision and unwavering dedication to reshaping our cities for the better.

Ramon Gras Alomà, adorned with degrees from BarcelonaTech, MIT, and Harvard, embodies a rare fusion of academia and entrepreneurship. As a City Science and Urban Design researcher at Harvard and the Co-founder of Aretian Urban Analytics and Design, his work transcends conventional boundaries, delving into the intricate nexus of technology, economics, and human flourishing within urban environments.

In his recent endeavour, "City Science: Performance Follows Form," Ramon offers a compelling narrative of urban dynamics, unpacking the hidden causal mechanisms that underpin the success or failure of cities in an era marked by technological revolution. This pioneering work serves as a beacon guiding urban planners, policymakers, and architects toward more informed, sustainable practices.

In our exclusive interview with Ramon Gras Alomà for Entrepreneur Prime magazine, we delve into the genesis of his entrepreneurial journey and the challenges encountered along the way. From the inception of Aretian to the validation of their ground-breaking methodologies, Ramon shares insights into the intricate dance between innovation and pragmatism in the realm of urban design.

Reflecting on the inception of Aretian, Ramon unveils a journey fuelled by a relentless pursuit of understanding urban complexities. His collaboration with Jeremy Burke birthed a methodology grounded in evidence-based complex systems, offering a novel lens to measure and evaluate urban success. Through empirical validation and accolades from prestigious institutions, Aretian swiftly garnered recognition, laying the foundation for transformative impact.

At the heart of Ramon's vision lies a profound commitment to societal well-being, encapsulated in Aretian's unique approach. With a diverse team of trailblazers and a steadfast focus on addressing critical urban challenges, Aretian stands as a beacon of innovation in the urban development landscape.

For aspiring entrepreneurs, Ramon offers sage advice rooted in the primacy of people and purpose. With a keen eye on the horizon, Aretian is poised to unveil its latest endeavour: a three-dimensional City Digital Twin. This revolutionary tool promises to revolutionize urban development, offering a scalable solution to navigate the complexities of modern cities.

As we navigate the urban tapestry of the future, Ramon Gras Alomà and Aretian Urban Analytics and Design emerge as guiding lights, illuminating a path towards sustainable, vibrant cities. Join us as we embark on a journey through the corridors of innovation and reimagine the cities of tomorrow, one visionary step at a time.

What inspired you to start your business?

In the Spring of 2018, I graduated from Harvard with a thesis on city science and urban design, aiming to inform sustainable development best practices in the face of the technology revolution driven by AI, automation, and robotics. The goal was to understand the deep, nontrivial causal mechanisms behind the success or failure of different cities and urban environments in order to create sustained prosperity cycles whilst raising the standard of living of citizens, in a context of high uncertainty in the global economy. My fellow co-founder Jeremy Burke and I worked together on designing an evidence-based complex systems methodology to model in a visual and mathematical way cities, urban environments, and architectural spaces, hence allowing us to measure and evaluate their success by means of Key Performance Metrics, illuminating structural and global patterns, and extracting insights to inform successful urban design and economic development strategies tailored for each society, context, and moment. We empirically validated a series core hypotheses by modeling first the US territory, then the World, thus allowing for creating a new model able to provide highly valuable recommendations and inform decision-making when addressing complex urban challenges worldwide.

What challenges did you find at the beginning of your journey and how did you overcome them?

We designed a new methodology (city science) for a early stage, nascent industry (city digital twins) in a new sector (smart cities), with a new team, so the first challenge was to prove the applicability of the new solution, and its ability to illustrate causal mechanisms, and to provide highly valuable insights that can raise the quality of decision making in urban design, architecture, civil engineering, economic development and real estate-related projects. The market tends to be sceptical about new solutions, and rather conservative. Thankfully, the more talented and brilliant our potential customers are, the more they understand and visualize the value of our contributions. A series of academic publications, and white paper reports, such as the Atlas of Innovation Districts, published in 2019 and announced by MIT Technology Review, provided visibility to our methods and grounded their scien-

Ramon Gras Alomà, co-founder of Aretian Urban Analytics and Design, illuminates the future of urban innovation through interdisciplinary vision and pioneering methodologies"

tific credibility. Happily, our team and projects received some awards from the Harvard Graduate School of Design (Excellence in Design Award), Harvard Office for Sustainability, BostInno, and the CogX / British academy for AI (Sustainable Cities and Communities Award), among others, as well as an interview at the Harvard Magazine contributed to disseminate the knowledge advances achieved by embracing this new methodology, and that helped us get our first clients in Boston, New York, and abroad.

How did you get the idea for your business and why did you think it would work?

We identified in our own professional practice in architecture, civil engineering and urban design a methodological gap that was hindering the ability for urban designers and city planners to address a series of key questions, such as how to address the needs of a specific community, and align aesthetics, functionality, and sustainability to create attractive and thriving communities. We drew inspiration from prior authors that we admire like Louis Durand, Ildefons Cerdà, Geoffrey West, Évariste Galois, Euler, or Eratosthenes, and their intuitions helped us conceive our core hypothesis, assumptions, and a vision of how the urban form, economic systems, and social dynamics can be modeled to describe mathematically how cities operative and what are the key ingredients and dynamics behind the success, economic dynamism, appeal, attractiveness and desirability of any human settlement around the globe. After endless brainstorming sessions and modeling efforts, the city science model was very robust, and provided us with the types of answers we wanted to address.

What kind of research did you do before you started?

We developed a thorough market research study to understand the needs of our potential client base across sectors such as urban design, city planning, economic development policymaking, real estate, and finance sectors: there really was an urgent need for more sophisticated ways of informing decision making processes for critical urban development projects . Besides, our work on urban innovation communities through the Atlas of Innovation Districts and

rural development needs such as the Aretian Agritechnology Campuses helped us ascertain the challenges that public administration and private investors constantly face when facing development challenges.

What motivates you to keep going? What makes your business unique?

The vision and methodology that we have designed is grounded on a fertile land and we continually advance our methods and solutions. We have a fantastic team, composed of highly talented, motivated and principled professionals, and we constantly strive for pushing the boundaries of the frontier of knowledge, aiming to provide a social service that can potentially have an immense impact on the quality of life, personal, and professional prospects of citizens worldwide. Such a compelling challenge is highly stimulating, and keeps a cohesive team and strengthens a shared ethos.

What advice would you give to someone who is trying to become an entrepreneur?

I would encourage them to primarily focus on the people, the team, and the social challenge they are addressing. A healthy, supportive work environment is critical for the success of any company, and the wellbeing of its employees.

What plans do you have for the future?

We are completing the design of a three-dimensional City Digital Twin, including a user-friendly web-based interface, that allows for addressing critical urban development challenges (urban design, smart specialization, innovation and talent development, mobility and logistics, housing and space programming) by performing four types of analyses: (1) highly detailed territorial SWOT diagnostics, (2) goal identification, (3) scenario planning and simulation, and (4) specific recommendations. The scalability of the solution is universal, and we think this new model can help address complex urban challenges at multiple scales, align the incentives of multiple stakeholders, and contribute to raise the quality of urban design practices around the globe.

Dr. Obioma Martin's Inspirational Journey Toward Transformation

Dr. Obioma Martin partners with SuccessBooks® to co-author "Against All Odds", offering resilience-filled narratives. Her leadership and advocacy uplift ndividuals worldwide.

In the dynamic world of entrepreneurship and leadership, alliances are forged, and collaborations are celebrated. This Summer of 2024 brings forth a collaboration of extraordinary minds as Dr. Obioma Martin joins forces with SuccessBooks® to co-author the eagerly awaited book, "Against All Odds", alongside the esteemed Lisa Nichols and a remarkable ensemble of authors.

Scheduled to hit the shelves soon, "Against All Odds" is poised to captivate readers with narratives brimming with resilience, fortitude, and tenacity, promising to inspire and uplift audiences worldwide.

Dr. Obioma Martin stands as a luminary in the realms of Early Childhood Education, Entrepreneurship, and Leadership. Her impressive repertoire includes titles such as business strategist, Accountability Coach, keynote speaker, Transformational Facili-

tator, and Lisa Nichols Certified Transformational Trainer. With a fervent dedication to nurturing growth and facilitating transformative learning experiences, Dr. Martin has cemented her position as a seven-time Amazon best-selling author and a compelling TEDx Speaker, touching countless lives with her poignant narratives and actionable insights.

At the helm of OMAX Institute, Dr. Martin leads the charge in the Center for Early Childhood Education, Entrepreneurship, and Leadership, empowering individuals to unleash their full potential. Through her leadership at OmazingYou, she advocates for the power of personal storytelling, enabling individuals to inspire and uplift others. Moreover, Dr. Martin's commitment to societal betterment shines through her founding of OMART Women Supporting Women, a nonprofit organization dedicated to aiding battered women with children and

teen parents.

Beyond her entrepreneurial ventures, Dr. Martin spearheads Obioma Martin LLC, leveraging her expertise in strategy and leadership to drive change and foster excellence. Her unwavering commitment to integrity, reliability, and dependability forms the cornerstone of her successful partnerships and professional endeavors.

Dr. Martin's academic credentials underscore her multifaceted approach to leadership and human relationships. With a doctorate in philosophy and certifications in trauma and biblical counseling, she embodies empathy and dedication to bringing healing and hope to those in need. As a John Maxwell certified leadership coach and speaker, she mentors emerging leaders, guiding them towards realizing their utmost potential.

In academia, Dr. Martin's scholarly prowess is reinforced

by master's degrees in early childhood education and leadership, positioning her as an esteemed authority in her domain. Her ordination as an evangelist reflects her commitment to spiritual service and her ability to inspire and guide her community through faith and wisdom.

Dr. Obioma Martin epitomizes the essence of transformational leadership—a beacon of hope, a catalyst for change, and a steadfast support for those defying all odds.

To delve deeper into Dr. Martin's journey and her forthcoming collaboration in "Against All Odds", visit Obioma.org.

SuccessBooks® warmly welcomes Dr. Obioma Martin as a co-author of "Against All Odds". Stay tuned for the release of this transformative book, poised to embolden and empower readers through the collective stories of Dr. Obioma Martin, Lisa Nichols, and an exceptional team of author

Katie J Design and Events Wins Best Kids Party Planner

Katie J Design and Events named Best Kids Party Planner/Stylist at the prestigious What's On 4 Kids Awards 2023-24.

Capturing the hearts and imaginations of families nationwide, Katie J Design and Events recently secured the coveted title of Best Kids Party Planner/Stylist at the prestigious What's On 4 Kids Awards 2023-24. With victories in both the 'People's Choice' and 'Judged' categories, the recognition underscores the unwavering dedication and passion of Katie Lynch and her talented team.

The journey of Katie J Design and Events began in 2014, when visionary Events Manager Katie Lynch embarked on a mission to transform the landscape of children's parties. Inspired by the joy of crafting personalized celebrations for her own children during maternity leave, Lynch's

endeavor quickly gained traction, leading to the establishment of Katie J Design and Events.

What sets Katie J Design and Events apart is its commitment to customer satisfaction and innovation. Offering over 400 meticulously curated party themes and designs through its online platform, the company has served over 25,000 delighted customers across Australia, ensuring precision and promptness in fulfilling orders.

In a bid to enhance user experience, Katie J Design and Events partnered with Customily in 2022, revolutionizing its online store and empowering customers to personalize and preview their own decorations. This innovative approach fosters a sense

of ownership and uniqueness, resonating deeply with clients seeking to create truly memorable experiences for their children.

Building upon this foundation of innovation, Katie J Design and Events introduced its latest breakthrough in 2023: the 'Create Your Own' party decorations range. This groundbreaking offering allows customers to infuse personality into their events by uploading custom designs or personal photographs onto premium-quality products, elevating the party-planning experience to new heights.

The What's On 4 Kids Awards, presented by Australia's leading "What's On 4 Kids" business, www.whatson4kids.com.au, are a testament to the excellence, pas-

sion, and commitment displayed by the kids activity industry in Australia. Each year, hundreds of small businesses across the country vie for recognition in various categories, showcasing the best in children's entertainment, education, and enrichment.

As the curtain falls on another remarkable edition of the What's On 4 Kids Awards, the spotlight shines brightly on Katie J Design and Events, a beacon of creativity, innovation, and excellence in the realm of children's parties. With a legacy of joyous celebrations and unforgettable memories, Katie J Design and Events continues to set the standard for excellence, inspiring families to dream, create, and celebrate together.

Women Leaders Share Their Best Advice With The Next Generation

Leading the Way: Insights from Wells Fargo's Female Powerhouses

Setting and reaching goals is never easy, and if you're a woman, you will likely face additional challenges on the path to achieving your dreams. But in the realm of banking, five remarkable women are breaking barriers and reshaping the industry. As honorees of American Banker's "Most Powerful Women in Banking," these leaders from Wells Fargo are not just paving the way; they're sharing invaluable advice with the next generation of female leaders.

TRACY KERRINS: STICK TO YOUR GOALS

Tracy Kerrins, Wells Fargo's head of technology, knows a thing or two about navigating obstacles. As one of the few women in a top tech role at a major American bank, Kerrins emphasizes the importance of persistence. "Stick to your goals, even when obstacles emerge, and rely on those who are truly inves-

ted in your success," she advises. Kerrins' strategic mindset keeps her ahead in a rapidly evolving tech landscape, where she's driving innovations to enhance the banking experience.

KRISTY FERCHO: CULTIVATE CURIOSITY

For Kristy Fercho, leading transformation in banking is not just a job—it's a mission. As head of diverse segments, representation, and inclusion at Wells Fargo, Fercho underscores the value of curiosity. "Be excellent at your job. Be curious. And most importantly: Be your authentic self," she advocates. Her commitment to diversity and inclusion fuels positive change within Wells Fargo and beyond.

ELLEN PATTERSON: LIFT OTHERS AS YOU RISE

Ellen Patterson, Wells Fargo's general counsel, credits her success to the collective effort of her team. Leading over 1,200 legal

professionals, Patterson believes in the power of collaboration and mentorship. "Be great at what you're doing, and actively look for ways to be helpful to those around you," she advises. Patterson's approach fosters a culture of support and excellence within her team.

TANYA SANDERS: INNOVATE SOLUTIONS

As head of Wells Fargo's auto division, Tanya Sanders combines banking expertise with a passion for problem-solving. With a background in mechanical engineering, Sanders sees challenges as opportunities for innovation. "There is incredible power in forging new and inclusive solutions," she asserts. Sanders encourages future leaders to collaborate and drive positive change for all.

KARA MCSHANE: MASTER THE ART OF COMMUNICATION

Kara McShane, head of Wells Fargo's commercial real estate division, understands the significance of effective communication in business. "Learn how to communicate clearly, concisely and confidently in order to be effective," she advises. McShane's emphasis on communication skills underscores their role in leadership success.

Whether you're a student, a recent graduate, or a seasoned professional, the wisdom shared by these outstanding women leaders can guide you through challenges and propel you towards success. By embracing their lessons, you can chart your own path to leadership and make a lasting impact in the banking industry and beyond.

Business Owners Are Optimistic as Economic Conditions Improve

What a difference a year makes. New research finds that small- and mid-sized business owners are increasingly optimistic about economic conditions and the prospects for their own businesses.

According to PNC's Spring 2024 Economic Outlook Survey, nearly 80% of business owners surveyed feel optimistic about conditions for their business over the next six months -- up from 60% a year ago.

This optimism likely stems from an improving outlook for the economy as a whole as inflation pressures and recession fears appear to be easing. A majority of those surveyed (55%) said they are highly optimistic about the national economy -- a dramatic increase from the 26% who felt that way in the spring of 2023. Even more (63%) said they are highly optimistic about their local economy -- more than double the reading from a year ago.

The uptick in optimism for the economy mirrors PNC's revised outlook for 2024, which shifts away from a predicted recession to a forecast of slow growth. PNC chief economist Gus Faucher said he expects the Federal Reserve will begin cutting interest rates later this year as inflation continues to ease.

"Business owners continue to feel confident that good days are ahead," Faucher said. "This time around though, the economy is seen as a supporting factor to that optimism instead of a limitation."

Calming Inflation

Easing inflation pressures are among the biggest factors reported in the survey. Last spring, 55% of respondents reported that they expected to raise prices in the ensuing six months -- that dropped to 47% this round. Similarly, 40% expect prices from suppliers to increase over the next six months, that's down from 47% last spring.

Inflation overall has been gradually easing since a mid-2022 high of 9% -- its highest level since the 1980s. By January 2024, inflation was reported at 3.1%, with continued easing projected in the months ahead. Still, inflation remains above its pre-pandemic pace and Faucher says more progress is needed before the Fed likely cuts rates later in 2024.

"We've come a long way from 2022, as supply chain issues driven by the pandemic have largely dissipated," Faucher said. "But more progress will probably be necessary before we can expect the Fed to start easing rates."

Labor Challenges Easing

One such challenge has been the tight labor market, which has made hiring difficult for business leaders. Consistent with PNC's Fall 2023 survey, respondents say the lack of overall applicants remains their primary hiring issue. Respondents cite lack of experience (22%) and high salary/benefit and flexibility requirements (9%) as other barriers.

The nationwide unemployment rate for January 2024 was 3.7% -- below what is considered "full employment" in the U.S. economy. Faucher said he expects the shortage of available labor to ease as consumer demand softens and the effect of slower job growth across the economy becomes more visible.

Despite the trend across the broader U.S. landscape, few survey respondents anticipate workforce reductions over the next six months. Only 4% report anticipating a reduction, while 74% expect no change to their workforce numbers and 21% project an increase in their workforce over the next half of the year.

"Employers have been under pressure despite the improving conditions because the economy has been at or near full employment for an extended period," Faucher said. "We expect some slack in the labor market in the coming months, which will likely further ease inflation." (StatePoint)

In the labyrinth of life's challenges, there often emerges a beacon of light, a soul whose journey transcends mere existence to embody resilience, reinvention, and profound purpose. Meet Crystal Johns, a visionary entrepreneur whose tale is as captivating as the radiant glow of her creations.

Crystal's odyssey began amidst the chaos of the Covid-19 pandemic, where she served tirelessly as a nurse within the NHS, navigating the stormy seas of burnout and stress. Yet, from the depths of adversity, she discovered a lifeline in therapy, piecing together the fragments of her fractured mental health. Despite the heartbreak of a shattered engagement, Crystal embarked on a quest for healing, guided by the mystical allure of crystals and the comforting embrace of twinkling lights.

From the ashes of despair rose Crystal's Healing Lights, a testament to her unwavering spirit and unwavering commitment to holistic wellness. Her journey is a symphony of serendipity and synchronicity, where personal growth intertwines seamlessly with entrepreneurial ambition.

Crystal's Healing Lights is not merely a business; it's a sanctuary, a haven of tranquillity where the radiant beauty of healing crystals converges with the soothing glow of light therapy. With each creation, Crystal invites us to embark on a journey of self-discovery, to illuminate our sacred spaces with the essence of peace and positivity.

Illuminating Tranquillity
The Journey of Crystal Johns and Crystal's Healing Lights

Crystal Johns, a resilient nurse turned entrepreneur, crafts tranquillity with Crystal's Healing Lights, blending healing crystals and light therapy. Her journey inspires hope and resilience amid life's turbulence.

In this exclusive interview with Entrepreneur Prime, Crystal unveils the secrets behind her entrepreneurial voyage, from the challenges of navigating uncharted waters to the profound lessons gleaned along the way. Through her words, we glimpse the essence of resilience, the power of perseverance, and the transformative potential of following one's heart.

As Crystal envisions a future where her entrepreneurial venture becomes a force for good, touching the lives of those in need, we are reminded of the boundless possibilities that await those who dare to dream. So, join us as we illuminate our lives with Crystal's Healing Lights and embark on a journey where tranquillity flows and dreams take flight.

Illuminate your soul. Embrace the magic. Welcome to the world of Crystal's Healing Lights.

What inspired your business?

My personal journey of healing, overcoming past traumas, resilience, the wedding centrepiece idea, all intertwined with my name. These elements guided me to the crystal shop, where I discovered my profound connection with healing crystals. In that serene space, I found a newfound passion that illuminated my path forward. Transforming my pain into my purpose. I discovered a profound sense of fulfilment in life.

What challenges did you find at the beginning of your journey and how did you overcome them?

Challenges. Not having access to the right business knowledge or mindset, not knowing my target audience, not accessing the right business courses, targeting the incorrect fairs/ shows and exhibitions. I didn't have a website to direct traffic to and I didn't understand pricing structures for material, costs and retail.

Overcome. I found business coaching which helped to guide me on the right path in terms of knowledge, mindset, courses and shows. By networking with other business owners and entrepreneurs I had a better understanding of sourcing and different pricing structures. After just over a year, I got up website up and running with the help of my web developer!

What kind of research did you do before you started?

The different crystal properties, including physical and emotional conditions, different chakras and star signs. Facts on how to pick/ choose crystals and how crystals are charged or cleansed. The best crystals for healing, work, meditation, study, love or marriage. Engaging crystal content for social media.

Researching my target audience, which professions use healing crystals, people with an interest in crystals, and which fairs or exhibitions would be best suited to my ideal customer.

The business side of it includes: social media, marketing, pricing, sourcing materials, and setting up my website and Etsy account.

What makes your business unique?

The unique sell point is centred around the crystal being part of the product design. These designs are protected. Combining the power of healing crystals and light therapy together in one wellness product.

What would you say to your old self?

Keep going don't stop. You have the power to work on yourself and grow- personally and professionally. You will make a positive impact in the world with your creations. Always listen to your intuition.

What do you envision for your entrepreneurial venture?

I would like to help two mental health charities. One of them is the CAMHS (Child and Adolescent Mental Health Service). I would like to contribute money to this service to help with children and young people's mental health. I worked as a children's nurse for ten years and seen a lot of deteriorating mental health. They need more funding to help shorten wait times.

I would like to set up a charity to help health care professionals access free and immediate mental health services, including therapy to address any past traumas in their lives. This cause is very close to my heart following my personal experience of burnout and stress after the pandemic.

It would also be great to contribute to an existing charity that would go in and spend time with the elderly to converse them. It can be quite a lonely place and this will also help to keep their mind stimulated to avoid the cognitive dip leading to Alzheimer's disease, as my grandma suffered with dementia in her later years.

Can you share a key lesson you've learned since starting your entrepreneurial journey? And how has it influenced your approach to business?

Be resilient, keep going, and don't give up. Remember, someone very wise once said, "Don't give up before you strike gold." In the midst of challenges and uncertainty, it's easy to feel discouraged, but every setback brings you clarity as you discover what works and what does not work.

I hold onto hope and perseverance; you never know when you're going to experience those breakthrough moments or opportunities, but when you do, it's all been worth it. I always remember who I am trying to help, my purpose, and the positive impact I am trying to make in the world.

Unveiling the World with

BORIS KESTER

Exploring Cultures, Unexpected Encounters, and the Essence of Global Exploration

Boris Kester, global adventurer, shares insights from visiting all 193 countries: surprising encounters, risky moments, and advice for aspiring travellers. His books capture the essence of exploration and curiosity.

In a world where borders are not just lines on a map but markers of identity, Boris Kester defies conventional boundaries with his insatiable

Boris Kester's global odyssey: exploring cultures, risking encounters, embracing transformation. From travel tales to literary endeavors, curiosity endures.

thirst for exploration. His journey is not merely about tallying passport stamps but about

unraveling the intricate threads that weave together the fabric of humanity itself. Through his remarkable odyssey, Boris has not only traversed the physical landscapes of 193 countries but has delved deep into the cultural tapestry of our planet, leaving behind a trail of stories that inspire and captivate.

In our exclusive interview with Boris Kester for Entrepreneur Prime magazine, we embark on a voyage beyond borders, guided by his unparalleled experiences and profound insights. From the remote corners of Kiribati to the vibrant streets of Gabon, Boris shares tales of unexpected encounters and daring escapades, offering a glimpse into the unpredictable essence of global

exploration.

As Boris reflects on his encounters and challenges, he unveils the transformative power of travel, urging aspiring adventurers to embrace the unknown with open minds and open hearts. His words resonate with the wisdom gained from years of traversing continents, reminding us to slow down, savor the moments, and immerse ourselves in the beauty of our world and its people.

Beyond the confines of his expeditions, Boris invites us into the realm of storytelling, where the challenge lies in distilling a lifetime of adventures into the pages of his acclaimed book, *The Long Road to Cullaville*. Yet, amidst his literary pursuits and ongoing adventures, Boris re-

mains anchored in the boundless allure of discovery, beckoning us to join him on a journey that transcends borders and defies expectations.

Join us as we embark on an extraordinary odyssey with Boris Kester, a modern-day explorer whose wanderlust knows no bounds and whose stories illuminate the vastness of our world and the endless possibilities that lie ahead.

What was the most surprising or unexpected encounter you had during your travels to all 193 countries?

Traveling in Kiribati (in the Pacific), I met a local guy who asked me where I was from. I told him, and since he didn't

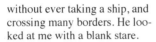

The Long Road to Cullaville - Boris Kester's captivating memoir chronicles his extraordinary adventures across the globe.

THE LONG ROAD TO CULLAVILLE

STORIES FROM MY TRAVELS TO EVERY COUNTRY IN THE WORLD

BORIS KESTER

SECOND EDITION

know the Netherlands, I said it was close to Germany, France, and the United Kingdom. He then asked me how many hours it would take me to get to Germany by boat. I was surprised, and explained that you take a car, train, or bicycle to get across the border. He didn't understand this, and then asked me how much time it would

Boris Kester's global journey transcends borders, embracing diverse cultures, unpredictable encounters, and the transformative power of exploration and storytelling.

take me to reach France by boat. Again, I told him that you can get to France by land and that there are no boats linking the two countries. I decided not to tell him that there's even another country, Belgium, separating the two. I went on to tell him that I could travel all the way to China

without ever taking a ship, and crossing many borders. He looked at me with a blank stare.

At first, I wondered how he could not know that most countries in Europe share land borders. Then, it dawned on me. This guy was from a nation of islands, in a region of islands. The island defines your identity. Bigger nations in the region are island nations, too: Philippines, Japan, New Zealand, Australia, Indonesia. Islands are clearly marked entities by nature. It put my whole project of visiting every country in a new perspective: I realized that borders are a human invention.

Can you share a particularly challenging or risky situation you encountered during your quest to visit every country?

When I refused to pay a bribe at a checkpoint in Gabon, and the (drunk) official didn't give me my passport, we ended up in a physical fight over the document. I was extremely fortunate that at exactly that moment, a convoy of vehicles passed by. The Minister of Justice happened to be in one of the vehicles, and he summoned both of us to talk to him. He made a call, and within twenty minutes, several police officers arrived. They sorted out the situation. I have always wondered what would have happened in case that minister wouldn't have passed by. Destiny (or sheer luck) is an important factor in both travel and life, and as such one of the themes of my book.

What advice would you give to aspiring travellers who want to embark on a similar journey to visit all the countries in the world?

I have two pieces of advice for them. First: leave your preconceptions at home. Embark on your journeys with an open mind, a curious mind, in which everything is possible. Be open to be surprised, and you will soon find out what an incredibly beautiful world we live in with equally beautiful people (most of the time). If you manage to travel this way, your travels will probably be the best teacher of life you ever had.

Secondly, I would tell all aspiring travellers to take it easy, and to take their time. I see quite a few travellers rushing through the world, ticking off countries, and I honestly don't see the sense of it. Enjoy your travels, take your time to get to know a country, to connect with people, to absorb what is happening around you. Travel is not competition, and if you don't make it to visit every country, that's perfectly fine.

How did writing your books differ from sharing your travel experiences on your website? Did you find it challenging to condense your adventures into book form?

I have shared my travel adventures since 25 years through my website traveladventures.org. Soon after visiting my last country, and completing my goal to visit every country in the world, I realized that the most exciting stories were hard or impossible to share through short stories on the internet. It was obvious that the best way to do so would be through a book. Anyway, it had been a child's dream to one day publish a book. Indeed, I loved the process of

writing. I had all the space I needed to tell my stories, and I worked hard to turn my travel adventures into literary words, as opposed to the internet where I write more like a reportage.

Now that you have visited all countries in the world, what's next?

I may have visited every country in the world, the main driving force behind my travels - curiosity - is still very much alive. I am still travelling like before, but without a clear goal in mind which, in a way, is liberating. I have a long list of places I want to visit. Through other travellers, I often get new ideas for places to visit. I do find, however, that I am avoiding touristy places. I am travelling to places where few people go, discovering obscure sites, enjoying breathtaking nature, while wondering why most people never get there.

Can we expect a second book from you?

Definitely! Shortly after my first book came out, I started writing my second one. First of all because many readers asked me for a sequel as they enjoyed the first book so much. Secondly, because I loved the writing process, and thirdly because I still have many more stories to share. My goal is to publish the second book in 2024. Besides, I am working on a third book as well, together with another traveller.

From Bulgaria to London.
Crafting Inclusive Luxury with Bibi Sakalieva

Explore Bilyana's journey from Bulgaria to London, crafting Bibi Sakalieva, a luxury fashion brand celebrating inclusivity and empowerment worldwide.

In the ever-evolving world of fashion, there are those who create garments, and then there are visionaries who craft experiences, narratives, and movements through their designs. Bilyana, the mastermind behind the luxury fashion brand Bibi Sakalieva, belongs firmly in the latter category. Born and raised in Bulgaria, Bilyana's journey from sewing clothes for her dolls to gracing the stages of London Fashion Week is a testament to her unwavering passion, creativity, and dedication to empowering women through fashion.

In this exclusive interview with Entrepreneur Prime, we delve into the captivating story of Bilyana and the brand she has built from the ground up. From her childhood fascination with fashion to the inception of Bibi Sakalieva and its meteoric rise in the competitive world of high-end fashion, Bilyana shares the inspirations, challenges, and triumphs that have shaped her remarkable journey.

At the heart of Bibi Sakalieva lies a commitment to inclusivity, ethical production, and celebrating the diversity of women's bodies and experiences. With each meticulously crafted garment, Bilyana seeks not only to adorn but to empower, offering women of all shapes, sizes, and backgrounds the opportunity to feel beautiful, confident, and seen.

Join us as we explore the intersection of artistry, culture, and empowerment with Bilyana, the visionary founder behind Bibi Sakalieva. Through her bold designs, inclusive philosophy, and global aspirations, she continues to redefine the boundaries of luxury fashion, proving that true style knows no boundaries.

Welcome to the world of Bibi Sakalieva, where fashion is not just a statement but a celebration of individuality, strength, and the enduring spirit of womanhood.

Bibi, as the founder of your eponymous brand, what inspired you to create a luxury fashion line that prioritizes empowering women and celebrating their unique identities?

I have always said that it's not what clothes you wear, but how you wear them. I kept hearing my friends admiring the women on the covers of magazines and my comment was: you can look like that if you ask.

Since then I have started designing clothes that look good on 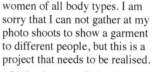 women of all body types. I am sorry that I can not gather at my photo shoots to show a garment to different people, but this is a project that needs to be realised.

Living between Bulgaria and London must provide you with a rich tapestry of cultural influences. How do these experiences inform the designs and aesthetic of Bibi Sakalieva's collections?

Oh yes, that concerns me very much. In London, I get inspired when I walk through the busy streets. As a multicultural capital, daily life there is very busy and full of diverse people expressing their roots. And as Bulgaria is a country with an ancient history, there is always something that inspires me from our folklore. So I try to design clothes that are suitable for the busy everyday life in London and add a little touch of my roots, be it in the form of an embroidery or a detail on a  garment.

Ethical production is a cornerstone of your brand. Could you walk us through the process of ensuring that each garment is ethically handmade in your Bulgarian atelier, and why this commitment is essential to you?

It's important to me that the people who work with me are paid a fair wage and are proud to be part of the creation process of the collection when it goes to market. That's why I try to pay the women in my team (currently there are two) a pretty good salary, in line with the standard in Bulgaria. We are not a fast fashion brand, so I do not design a new collection every 4 months.

You've made a bold choice to move away from traditional sizing and instead design clothes to fit all shapes and sizes. Can you share some insights into how you approach this inclusive design philosophy and the impact it has had on your customers?

I do not know how, but somehow I can tell a body if it will look good in a certain outfit. Like I said, my clients and friends always have something they do not like about themselves. I do not know how, but somehow I can tell a body if it will look good in a certain outfit. I had a case with a client who was not up to standard and came to me asking me to help her.

PHOTO: Bilyana, founder of Bibi Sakalieva, brings her vision to life, celebrating diversity and empowerment through each meticulously crafted garment."

EMPOWERING ELEGANCE::: *"Bibi Sakalieva's designs grace the runway, embodying elegance and celebrating the beauty of diversity with every model adorned."*

I suggested making one of our pleated wide leg trousers for her but changing the width of the belt. She was quite sceptical because she is small and weighs more than the accepted standards. I told her she could return it if she didn't like it. A week after receiving her order, the customer came to me overjoyed and told me how many compliments she had received at an event where she wore our wide-leg trousers, all from men.

I'd also venture to say that some of my styles look very good on women with mastectomies. I met a woman who has lived through this nightmare and wants to create collections for these women with the help of designers. She tried on one of my jumpsuits and we saw that it fits very well. Now I'm going to work with her to improve the cut of this garment a little and make it fit better for these women who have been through the nightmare of breast cancer.

In a world where beauty standards can be restrictive, how does Bibi Sakalieva aim to redefine beauty and confidence through fashion, and what message do you hope to convey to women who wear your designs?

So I'm designing clothes that are feminine and slightly flamboyant, that are suitable for the modern woman, the mum, the housewife, the woman who goes out to work, looks after her family and tries to have a social life. A garment that she can wear everywhere. A garment that makes her feel noticed, beautiful and boosts her self-esteem

Looking towards the future, what are your aspirations for Bibi Sakalieva? How do you plan to continue championing inclusivity and individuality in the luxury fashion industry while expanding your brand's

reach?

My endeavours are aimed at discovering the needs of customers in different markets and offering these to them. For example, I've an offer from a boutique in Hong Kong, but I need to remodel and redesign some of my designs with fabrics and cuts that are suitable for that market.

Bibi, participating in events like Pure London can provide invaluable opportunities for networking and exposure within the fashion industry on a global scale. How has your experience at Pure London contributed to shaping your brand's global aspirations, and what insights or predictions do you have regarding the direction of fashion trends and consumer preferences in the coming years?

Taking part in Pure London has its advantages for every brand. Of course, interest in new names is increasing, as is interest in sustainable fashion. More and more customers and department stores' chains are focusing on sustainable fashion. I also met a partner at Pure London who offered to test my denim collection on the Scandinavian market. So there will be a lot to do in the coming months.

Available both print and electronic all over the globe.
Entrepreneur Prime reaches more then 40.000
retailers (including Amazon, Barnes & Noble
Waterstones, Blackwells, and local independent
bookstores in the United States.)

Visit entrepreneurprime.co.uk for more

entrepreneur prime

Save up to 50% when you
order 10 or more from the
same issue

Milton Keynes UK
Ingram Content Group UK Ltd.
UKHW050403010424
440200UK00001B/2